Columbia University

Contributions to Éducation

Teachers College Series

No. 778

AMS PRESS
NEW YORK

SKETCHING THE NORRIS DAM

Outcomes of a Study Excursion

A DESCRIPTIVE STUDY

By James Anderson Fraser

SUBMITTED IN PARTIAL FULFILLMENT OF THE REQUIREMENTS
FOR THE DEGREE OF DOCTOR OF PHILOSOPHY IN THE
FACULTY OF PHILOSOPHY, COLUMBIA UNIVERSITY

*Published with the Approval of Professor Irving Lorge
and Professor Herbert J. Arnold, Co-sponsors*

BUREAU OF PUBLICATIONS

TEACHERS COLLEGE, COLUMBIA UNIVERSITY

NEW YORK

1939

Library of Congress Cataloging in Publication Data

Fraser, James Anderson, 1907–
    Outcomes of a study excursion.

    Reprint of the 1939 ed., issued in series: Teachers
College, Columbia University. Contributions to educa-
tion, no. 778.
    Originally presented as the author's thesis, Columbia.
    Bibliography: p.
    1. School excursions. 2. Columbia University.
Teachers College. Lincoln School. I. Title. II. Se-
ries: Columbia University. Teachers College. Contri-
butions to education, no. 778.
LB1047.F7 1972   371.3'8   75-176785
ISBN 0-404-55778-3

Reprinted by Special Arrangement with Teachers
College Press, New York, New York

From the edition of 1939, New York
First AMS edition published in 1972
Manufactured in the United States

AMS PRESS, INC.
NEW YORK, N. Y.   10003

ACKNOWLEDGMENTS

As CO-SPONSORS of this study, Professors Irving Lorge and Herbert J. Arnold have contributed the encouragement, the critical judgment, and the understanding guidance which made it possible. The association with these men has been a pleasure and a privilege. To Professor Lorge special acknowledgment is made for his unfailing guidance in the technical aspects of the study. Professors S. Ralph Powers and Lester Dix gave freely of most helpful advice and encouragement.

This study would have been impossible without the friendly co-operation and unfailing assistance of Lawrence Riggs, Edwin S. Fulcomer, Miss Elmina R. Lucke, Miss Alice Schoelkopf, Mrs. Satis N. Coleman, Henry Courtenay Fenn, and G. Derwood Baker, all of the Lincoln School; and the boys and girls of the 1937–1938 American Culture class.

Grateful acknowledgment is made to the following specialists who co-operated in the capacities of experts and raters for the determination of the scoring keys: Professors Paul B. Sears, George T. Renner, Jr., George W. Hartmann, Harold F. Clark, O. S. Morgan, Edmund deS. Brunner, John E. Orchard, Robert von Nardroff, F. W. Hehre, W. I. Slichter, J. W. Russell, G. W. De Harness, Herbert J. Arnold, Harold W. Webb; Miss C. M. Bergen, Miss W. Hill, Mr. W. Lyle Brewer, Mr. Frederick T. Howard. Dr. H. Emmett Brown, Mr. Warren W. McSpadden, Mr. Widnell D! Knott, Mr. William O. Stanley, Mr. Ebrahim Meratt, and Mr. Kenneth Dean Benne.

Valuable assistance in the form of critical judgment and helpful suggestions has been received from friends, too numerous to list, in the Advanced School of Education of Teachers College, Columbia University.

To my wife, Nina Rust Fraser, grateful acknowledgment is made for inspiration, encouragement, and assistance.

The unfailing confidence of my mother and father, Mr. and Mrs. Kenneth Fraser, has continually been a source of strength.

J. A. F.

CONTENTS

CONTENTS

Outcomes of a Study Excursion

A DESCRIPTIVE STUDY

CHAPTER I

THE PROBLEM

INTRODUCTION

THE study excursion as an educational procedure is not new. Good teachers, desirous of vitalizing their work through direct experience with the problems and situations under consideration, have long turned to it as an effective educational enterprise. Despite rather widespread and growing use, little has been done to determine the outcomes of such excursions by the techniques of recognized evaluation procedures. Aside from a study by Atyeo [3 : 1–194] * and one by Grinstead [13], both of which will be described in Chapter II, very little material in the field of objective evaluation of study excursions is available. Literature stating purposes, administrative procedures, and subjective evaluations is abundant.

With the growth of interest in general education, and the consequent enlargement of educational purposes, the study excursion is gaining recognition as one procedure for attaining the objectives which general education recognizes. Lincoln School of Teachers College, aware of the possibilities of this method, undertook during the academic year of 1937–1938 a rather ambitious program involving numerous experimental excursions. Among these was one undertaken by the senior class in American Culture to study National and Regional Planning.

The writer, whose major interest lies in the contribution which science and science education have to offer to the broader field of general education, was associated with the senior class in the capacity of science consultant. Since the study excursion was planned on an experimental basis, and since evaluation should be an integral part of any learning experiment, the present investigation was planned to

* The number in brackets before the colon refers to the bibliographical reference of that number, and the numbers after the colon, to pages in that reference.

measure certain of the possible outcomes and to study some relationships among them.

DEFINITION OF STUDY EXCURSION

The expression "study excursion" is used in the present report to designate any kind of expedition or trip, definitely organized to achieve certain objectives for young people, and made by a group of students as part of their regular school work. Such definition of the expression excludes consideration of unplanned and unorganized excursions where objectives are vague or absent. It also excludes consideration of excursions planned primarily for recreation or pleasure. In order to be included within the definition, a study excursion must be carefully planned, preferably co-operatively, to meet clearly stated objectives. This planning will usually result in three broad phases: (1) preparation, (2) the excursion, (3) the follow-up study. However, if the excursion is used largely as motivation for study and in consequence is undertaken before planning or preparatory study, it is equally worthy of consideration under the above definition. Atyeo [3 : 6] defines "school excursion" to mean essentially the same as the above. His definition is as follows:

The expression "school excursion" is used in the present study to designate any kind of definitely organized trip with a primarily educational purpose, made by a group of pupils as part of their regular school work.

With these limitations upon the use of the expression, it becomes necessary to justify its use in connection with the Lincoln School senior class study excursion.

TEACHING AND LEARNING PROCEDURES

The philosophy of the Lincoln School senior class in American Culture will be elaborated in Chapter II. The purpose of this section is to explain the class organization and the procedures employed.

Twenty boys and twenty-six girls, regularly enrolled in the senior class, participated in the study excursion. The teaching procedures may be divided into three parts for purposes of exposition: (1) the preparatory study, (2) the excursion, (3) the follow-up study.

The preparatory study started on Monday, January 3, 1938, and ended on Friday, January 28. During this time individual teachers were working with the class as follows:

General organization: G. Derwood Baker.
Planning for transportation, residence and food: Elmina R. Lucke.
Overview of the anticipated science problems: James A. Fraser.
Overview of the literature of the regions to be visited: Edwin S. Fulcomer.
Overview of the social problems involved in "planning": Lawrence Riggs.
Music, including study of that characteristic of the regions to be visited and practice of choral work to be used as the group's contribution to others' enjoyment: Satis N. Coleman.
Art, including techniques and material expected to be necessary: Alice Schoelkopf.

A battery of pre-tests designed for evaluation of some of the study excursion outcomes was administered before the preparatory study began. When the tests were taken, the class was divided into two sections: one to study the science problems of land management, power production, and flood control, which were to be encountered; the other to study social problems, such as government vs. private ownership of utilities, purposes and achievements of national and regional planning, and community problems characteristic of the regions to be visited. These two sections alternated study periods, so that each section worked for one period each day on each aspect of the preparatory study. At times both sections met together to discuss common problems. All participating teachers were present at such discussions, and each contributed from his store of specialized information. During some periods, the entire class practiced singing. During others, they studied literature and art, all relative to the understanding and appreciation of anticipated experiences on the excursion.

The students participated, through committees, in the planning of both the study and the administrative aspects of the excursion. The following student committees were formed:

Organization and Administration
People of the Tennessee Valley and Regions We Visit
Philosophy of Planning
Power Production, Distribution and Use
Soil Conservation
Education in the Tennessee Valley Region
Community Planning
Labor
Geological and Natural Resources

These functioned with the guidance of an appropriate staff member.
The following outline of procedures was developed in staff conference with the assistance of student discussion. It was mimeographed and distributed to the students on January 4.

TWELFTH GRADE COURSE, LINCOLN SCHOOL

A STUDY OF NATIONAL AND REGIONAL PLANNING

PROCEDURES

In our study of the TVA it will be necessary to follow certain procedures in order to facilitate matters generally. That you may know more
fully what to expect, the following is given as a general outline (subject
to change only if necessary).

1. *Class presentations* and discussions will be conducted on the assump-
   tion that you have read the previously assigned materials or have done
   to the best of your ability whatever the assignment calls for.

2. There will be required *basic reading assignments* for everyone. In some
   cases there will be extra requirements in reading to get a more satisfactory background. *Supplementary reading* and *enrichment reading* will
   be suggested and made available, but not assigned specifically.

3. There will be *frequent quizzes and occasional tests* to be considered as
   learning aids, as individual opportunities to check up on essential things
   and as evidence of your personal progress and achievement.

4. Everyone will be asked to keep a *working vocabulary* for personal frequent reference and a *bibliography* of all materials covered beyond the
   basic assignments. Details of these will be discussed in due time.

5. Aside from participating in the regular class work each individual will
   find at least two other jobs to be done:
   a. One will be in the nature of *participating on a committee* responsi-

ble for the closer examination and study of a special phase of our general study.

  b. The other will be an *individual selection and major study* surveying as completely as possible some topic that can be studied more fully because of the trip. It is hoped that a creative and authoritative presentation of his subject will be made by each student. This item will be completed after our trip but must be started before then. More on this later when the assignment will be made.

6. On the trip *diary records* will be kept in addition to certain notes you will need. *Pictures and sketches* will be invaluable.

7. On our return we will spend several weeks in a *follow-up* study and in gaining more historical perspective about the factors we find to be involved.

Keep in mind that we are each involved in a rare opportunity for learning, but let us not forget that more important than acquiring facts is our ability to learn to think about those facts, to form intelligent opinions and creative attitudes so that we may act as better informed persons and citizens.

There will be an extraordinary demand on each of us to be our most expert selves in matters of co-operation, understanding and respect for persons. Here is a chance seldom had by a group such as our class to develop expertness in human relationships.

Your teachers are desirous of helping you, advising you and learning with you but they cannot learn for you. That job is up to you as an individual. May we all find satisfaction, happiness and success in accomplishing it!

On January 18, the following student committees were formed to function during the actual excursion: Itinerary, Correspondence, Social, Baggage, Housing, Courtesy. One staff member acted as adviser to each.

It should be emphasized that indoctrination concerning any side of a controversial social issue was minimized through assignment and suggestion of reading materials which presented many different points of view, and through the fact that the teachers comprising the staff, although informed on the subjects, were not in agreement in their attitudes toward the issues involved.

The excursion started on Friday, January 28, at 7:30 p. m. The group traveled from New York City to Roanoke, Va., in two reserved

Pullman coaches on the Pennsylvania Railroad. From Roanoke travel was effected through the use of two Greyhound busses. A short stop at the plant and housing development of the American Bemberg Corporation broke the day's journey to Norris, Tenn.

Living in dormitories formerly used by engineers and other construction workers, the group studied in the vicinity of Norris from Saturday evening, January 29, until Tuesday, February 1.

From the dormitories, the group made short journeys to study the dam, the power house, the Norris school, the ceramic laboratory, the hydraulics laboratory, and the nursery, and to hear lectures by government officials. The teaching procedures during the excursion were informal and spontaneous. In the bus, teachers assisted students to interpret observations as they were made. At Norris, teachers assisted students to understand the technicalities of lectures and explanations given by officials; e.g., the engineer who explained the principles and practice of power production at the Norris dam used some terms which were not known to the students. It was the writer's function to clarify these during informal discussions with small groups.

The same informality of instruction was continued throughout the excursion. En route to the next major stop, Clarkesville, Ga., the class visited the plant of the Georgia Power Company, at Tallulah, Ga. They thus had an opportunity to compare the plant owned by a private power company with one owned by the government, and to compare the social arguments of the government with those of private officials and of the people served by government and private power plants.

On a farm near Clarkesville, owned by Dr. M. Mitchell, the group experienced the problems of land management. For two days, working parties under the direction of experienced farmers from the district, with the assistance of staff members, worked at the various tasks necessary to build a planned farm from one where soil depletion had resulted from lack of land management. All students in turn cut brush, built fences, cleared land, plowed, repaired and redecorated a farmer's house, surveyed land for contour plowing and terracing, surveyed land for construction of a dam, ran a terracing machine, spread lime and phosphate, and ground corn in an old mill.

Many of them lived with local farmers, and thus were able to experience the problems of living in a soil-eroded area. Informal discussions in which students, staff, officials, students from New College, local boys and girls, and even newspaper reporters participated, were the teaching procedures which supplemented direct experience.

The return journey was made to Williamsburg, Va., via Hoffman, N. C. At Hoffman, another Land Use Project was studied. An evening was spent at the Hampton Institute. The excursion concluded on Tuesday, February 8, with a visit to the Greenbelt Housing Project, just outside Washington, and the return trip on the Congressional Limited from Washington to New York City.[1]

The follow-up study began on February 9 and continued until March 16. Teaching procedures included class discussions of experiences, debates, short lectures by teachers, and library research. The class divided into committees according to their expressed interests for the purpose of studying carefully some problem which had challenged them during the excursion. Teachers directed the study activities of these committees.

LIMITATIONS AND PURPOSES OF THE STUDY

It was stated above that the present investigation was planned to measure certain of the possible outcomes and to study some relationships among them. Those outcomes and relationships were as follows:

1. Growth in understanding of the problems of soil erosion and land management, and growth in understanding of the procedures and processes used to convert energy of falling water into useful electrical energy.

2. Changes in attitude toward the following public problems:
   a. Public relief.
   b. Unlimited individual initiative in farming.
   c. Socio-economic planning.
   d. Conservation.
   e. Private ownership of utilities.

[1] Readers interested in the many details of administration are referred to a Teachers College Doctor of Education Project report-in-progress, by G. Derwood Baker. [4]

3. Changes in opinions regarding the following propositions:
   a. An individual farmer should possess the sole right to make decisions in regard to the farming practice on his own farm.
   b. It is wise for the government to lead in the development of the kinds of socio-economic planning carried on in the Tennessee Valley.
   c. It is wise for the government to enter the power business in competition with existing private power companies.
   d. Communism, civil war, people's fronts, national governments, and central economic planning, are all different forms of a revolt against private monopolies.
   e. Planning is not something new; it is the very stuff of which civilization has been made.
   f. We are sure to have for the next generation an increasing contest between those who have and those who have not.
   g. Governments should come to the assistance of people who have low standards of living, even if those people are not enthusiastic about receiving such assistance.
4. Growth in ability to identify evidence of poor land management and procedures for better land management.
5. Growth in ability to recognize the application of principles of land management.
6. Growth in ability to recognize the application of principles of power production.
7. Growth in ability to generalize in regard to land management.
8. Growth in ability to generalize in regard to power production.
9. Evidences of other growths, such as in reflective thinking and in personal relationships.

The above possible outcomes and relationships are by no means an exhaustive list. Obviously many other growths might occur on a study excursion, such as the one with which this report is concerned. To attempt the measurement of all possible growths would be to attempt a task so large as to defy completion. The possible outcomes selected have been selected because they are ones which the advocates of general education claim to be important. Thus the results of this study should throw light on the value of the study excursion as an instrument for attaining the purpose of general education. The study did not attempt to discover what particular aspects of the total experience offered to the group were responsible for each of the outcomes observed.

SUMMARY

The problem with which this report is concerned is that of evaluating certain of the possible outcomes of the 1938 Lincoln School senior class study excursion to Tennessee and Georgia. For the purposes of this report, study excursion is defined as any kind of expedition or trip definitely organized to achieve certain objectives for young people, and made by a group of students as part of their regular school work. The Lincoln School senior class study excursion meets the requirements of this definition in that it was definitely organized to achieve certain objectives. This was effected through protracted study of National and Regional Planning. The study excursion was made during school time, as part of the regular school work. The teaching and learning procedures were characterized by informality, student participation, purposeful activity, emphasis upon social problems, provision for individual differences and interests, attention to the development of critical thinking, and attempts to develop generalizations.

CHAPTER II

GENERAL EDUCATION AND THE STUDY EXCURSION

THIS thesis is oriented in the belief that general education embodies a philosophy of education which gives needed direction to trends in educational practice. It is the author's belief that the study excursion is one method for implementation of the aims of general education. Study excursions may be exceedingly valuable in attaining the purposes of vocational education, professional education, or other types of special education. This report, however, is not concerned so much with the study excursion as a technique for attaining the purposes of these special forms of education as it is with it as a technique for attaining the purposes of general education. If some of the objectives of general education can be achieved through the study excursion, one might expect the technique to achieve some objectives of special education.

GENERAL EDUCATION

Statements of the purposes of general education vary to such an extent that it seems necessary to specify which scheme of general education is being considered. The concept of general education in which this study is oriented is the result of the writer's interpretation of the work of the committee appointed to consider a projected proposal for an enlarged program for general education—a committee appointed in the fall of 1936 by the Dean of Teachers College, Columbia University. The committee included representatives from the social sciences, literature, the arts, home economics, and science.[1] The original statement of the aim of general education as presented by this committee in its progress report [21 : 8] is as follows: "The function of general education is to bring the individual into contact with the cul-

[1] The appointees were Dr. Karl Bigelow, visiting Professor of Education (social science); Dr. Helen Judy-Bond, Associate Professor of Household Arts; Dr. Lennox B. Grey, Assistant Professor of English; Dr. James L. Mursell, Associate Professor of Education (arts). Dr. S. Ralph Powers, Professor of Natural Sciences and Director of the Bureau of Educational Research in Science, served as chairman.

ture which is his birthright in such fashion as to widen and deepen
his consciousness of his relation to the life of the past, the present,
and the future, and to aid in the development of those attributes
which are most needed if he is to play intelligently his personal role
in the drama of cultural continuance and cultural change. Such attributes include certain skills, attitudes, interests, habits and understandings, vitally and integrally related to one another, and suited to
the continuous service of the individual's needs as well as of the
needs of the society of which he is a member."

This, with accompanying analysis of aims and purposes, furnishes
a clear and positive statement of trends in the current emphasis
on general education. It emphasizes the need for vital contact with
the culture and insists that the contact be such as to widen and deepen
the individual's consciousness of his relation to life. It stresses
individual growth, not subject matter per se. Information about subject matter and skill in manipulation of subject matter are not glorified as the only objectives, or as the primary objectives of educational
experiences. While knowledge and its acquisition are not the whole
of education, knowledge is basic for well oriented thinking, well
founded attitudes, and well established appreciations. General education does not minimize knowledge. It makes explicit, however,
some objectives which have either been implicit in education, or
which have not been considered. It stresses in addition to facts and
skills, the development of understandings in generalization and in application of information and of skill, and the engendering of attitudes, appreciations, and interests of the learner in relation to his
society. Information, skill, generalizations, application, interests, attitudes, appreciations, should be developed in such a way as maximally to realize the potentialities of the learner in reference to the
needs of the society that is and that is to be. The definition, while not
precise in terms of classroom practice, is valuable as a statement of
the general purpose to be served.

Such aims have been given form in a report entitled "A Program
for Science Education," which was prepared by Professor S. Ralph
Powers of Teachers College, Columbia University, for the General
Education Board. The Board granted financial assistance and a "Bu-

reau of Educational Research in Science" was established at Teachers College in September, 1934. The aims of the Bureau have been [22 : 3]: "(*a*) to examine and evaluate, through the use of suitable criteria, proposed objectives for instruction in science in general education, (*b*) to formulate a program for instruction in science in general education, consistent with the objectives most approved by modern educational thought, (*c*) to select and organize scientific materials which represent the best contemporary knowledge and which are best suited to use in such a program as that just described, and (*d*) to check the efficiency of teaching methods by studying the changes which occur in learners of differing degrees of maturity as a result of various educational experiences." Of course, some of these same goals had been suggested earlier. In a recent article, John Dewey draws attention to the evils of isolating subjects from their social setting, and clearly presents one of the practices to which general education is a constructive reaction:

When I asked how far the social is from an educational point of view the limiting function of all the studies, the question I had in mind was whether such subjects as, for example, the history, geography and natural science already mentioned can be isolated so as to be treated as independent subjects; or whether from the beginning, and constantly, they should be treated in their social bearings and consequences—consequences in the way, on one side, of problems and on the other side of opportunities. The human and cultural is after all the embracing limit to which all other things tend. In the higher reaches of school education there must, of course, be provision for training of experts and specialists. In them a certain amount of relative separation of subjects from their social context and function is legitimate. But it is a fair question whether society is not suffering even here because the expert specialists have not the educational background which would enable them to view their special skills and knowledge in connection with social conditions, movements and problems.

But the particular point which I would make is that in any case we have carried the isolation of subjects from their social effects and possibilities too far down the educational scale. From the psychological and moral standpoint it may be urged that for most boys and girls the material of studies loses vitality, becomes relatively dead, because it is separated from situations, and that much of the need which is felt at the present time for resorting to extraneous devices to make subjects interesting or else to coerce attention is a necessary effect of this isolation.

The study excursion is one of the means proposed by many educators to prevent the isolation of "the history, geography and natural science" and to treat them, "in their social bearings and consequences —consequences in the way, on one side of problems and on the other side of opportunities."

The emphasis upon contemporary society as both the source and the method of education is again illustrated by the authors of *The Educational Frontier* [8 : 52–53]:

> This is not the place to consider in detail the nature of modifications going on in family life, in sex relations, in the church, business, commerce, finance, the press, the theatre, and organized sport, government and politics, because of the impact of science and technology. And yet the substantial material and effective method of teaching must be determined on this basis. Otherwise a philosophy of education emphasizing social concepts will inevitably become formal and tend to be an affair of phraseology without specific bearing on the conduct of the educational system.

With educational unity as its goal, general education does not focus its attention on the individual alone, or upon society alone, but upon the functioning individual in a changing society. For such a goal, experiences are planned which will tend to develop in the individual the skills, interests, habits, attitudes, appreciations, and understandings which are essential for that individual to take his place in the modern world effectively. Special emphasis is conceded to the educational value of broad generalized insights. L. K. Frank expresses the thought as follows [10 : 173]:

> Here general education faces a fascinating but almost unique task since it is not detailed knowledge of facts and figures, nor skill in using techniques nor mastery of current theories, that is the burden of general education, as contrasted with the training of future astronomers, geologists, paleontologists, and biologists; the essential task is to convey some of the general ideas, meanings, and significances of these sciences to those who are in need of a new framework of beliefs to replace those that have been destroyed. The need of youth and of adults is for coherent, interrelated ideas, conceptions, and meanings drawn from and solidly supported by scientific research, but presented so that they are meaningful and congruent.

Methods proposed for achieving this broad aim are legion. This fact must obtain because of the variety of interests, needs, capacities, and opportunities of individuals and the variety of emphases upon social needs in different communities. However, some methodological trends are characteristic of the movement. Among these are: (*a*) plans which aim to help the teachers understand the needs, interests, and capacities of each pupil; (*b*) development of survey courses with generalizations as their aim; (*c*) attention to critical scientific problem solving; (*d*) special attention to contemporary problems of society and of the pupil in society; (*e*) a search for procedures which will encourage diligent, purposeful effort to understand current social problems.

THE STUDY EXCURSION

It would be extravagant to claim that the study excursion is a procedure which is exclusively designed for the purposes of general education in a democracy. Countries such as Germany, with social philosophies which differ markedly from democracy, find it useful. Atyeo [3 : 41] in a comprehensive study of the excursion as a teaching technique finds that "Germany and England have been leaders in the use of the educational excursion. Its acceptance as a method of instruction has both encouraged and been encouraged by the hostel movements, which have made suitable inexpensive accommodations available for journeys of some duration." He also finds [3 : 41] that "The method is employed more or less extensively in other European countries—in Austria, France, Italy, Russia, Poland, and in Japan. In most of the countries which have been studied, the excursion is handled so as to fit into the national educational pattern and contribute to the fulfillment of the national aim."

It would not be just to claim that the study excursion is a specially designed instrument of general education. However, the values claimed for excursions are such that they are in some cases identical with, and in other cases easily adapted to, the purposes of general education in a democracy.

Atyeo [3 : 189] summarizes the values of excursions in the following words:

A very wide range of values is claimed for the excursion technique in the literature. The power of the excursion to increase interest, deepen capacity for appreciation, develop accuracy and keenness in observing, secure a longer retention of knowledge acquired by its means, provide opportunity for development of initiative, leadership, sense of responsibility, independence of judgment, and to afford experience with social adjustments involved in planning and carrying out a group enterprise—all of these and many more recur repeatedly, expressed in many different ways, among the advantages attributed to the method.

Comparison of these values claimed for the excursion with the purposes of general education will reveal similarities in values and of objectives.

Atyeo further states [3 : 5]: "It is in its as yet unmeasured social values that the excursion may claim to take precedence over the laboratory as a means of introduction to the world in which the child must live." Here, he claims for the excursion a value which has been shown to be among the major purposes of general education.

In the spring of 1932, R. H. Price [23 : 302–305] received in answer to a questionnaire replies from 268 principals of public schools regarding the extent to which public schools participated in excursions. He concluded that too little use was being made of the method, but found that the principals recognized the following values as inherent in it:

1. Enriches curriculum with real experiences.
2. Makes school activities more meaningful.
3. Broadens interests.
4. Provides sources of direct information.
5. Affords opportunities for choosing, planning, executing and evaluating.

Here again is a set of claimed values which approximate those sought by the proponents of general education.

Crawford and Grinstead [6 : 301–306] list the following advantages of the excursion method:

1. The excursions are of more interest to students than are the more bookish types of classroom procedure.

2. They give education a decidedly practical direction since they involve a study of the realities of life. In other words they help to bridge the gulf between the school and the world in which we live.
3. Well chosen trips afford valuable vocational or educational guidance by offering the students a chance to explore and become acquainted with a wide range of occupational activities.
4. The excursions provide a useful fund of experience and mental imagery for the interpretation of the abstract materials of books.
5. A single excursion may provide experiences which will be of value in the understanding of a number of different subjects besides the one of which the excursion was a part.

The emphasis upon interest which results from setting the educational experience in broad relationships, in "situations" as Dewey says, is consistent with the aims of general education. So, too, are the advantages listed as numbers 2 and 3 above.

Arnold [2 : 13], in recognition of the value of study excursions as an educational technique, accepts as the threefold purpose of his study:

First, to select the major generalizations from the field of geology which may be of interest to liberally educated persons. Second, to develop a technique for the selection of localities and materials suitable for the illustration of these generalizations. Third, to discover what materials and localities are available within a reasonable distance of New York City for the illustration of these generalizations.

THE LINCOLN SCHOOL STUDY EXCURSION

The general course at the twelfth-grade level in Lincoln School is concerned with the study of the American social scene of the present day. Its purposes approximate the purposes of general education. They are to aid the individual to develop with a deeper appreciation of the life in which he lives, and to aid the group to develop the largest number possible of mutual understandings in common experiences. Subject matter is not emphasized as an end in itself. Instead the needs and purposes of each individual student are made the basis for determining his classroom activities. The teachers accept the challenge which arises from the conflict of the individual with social pressures. Considerable importance is given to the development of attitudes, habits, and skills which will help the individual to adjust continually to a changing social environment. Edwin S. Fulcomer [11 : 426], staff president of the experimental group used in this study, confirms this when he says:

They [the students of the grade twelve American Culture class] then feel the real thrill of learning and they are well on their way toward the acquisition of the attitudes and some of the skills of the self-educating personality. To the extent that all Lincoln School graduates reach this stage, the work of the staff will have been fully justified.

The students who participated in the Lincoln School study excursion were those in the American Culture class. Lincoln School is one of the thirty experimental schools under the Aikin Committee on the Relation between School and College of the Progressive Education Association. Its graduates are thus exempted from meeting the traditional college entrance requirements, and thus the curriculum may be planned to meet the aptitudes and interests of the students. The school recognizes that aptitudes and interests can best be served when the teachers recognize in their daily work that they cannot serve either the individual or the society without serving both. Education is recognized as a social service which draws its patterns and purposes from the group it serves. Lester Dix, Principal of Lincoln School, says [9 : 366], "There is no insulated vacuum in which can be erected a structure of education purified of social meanings, causes and effects."

With this philosophy and organization the American Culture class unhesitatingly grasped the opportunity offered by Alfred P. Sloan, when he allotted a sum of money to Lincoln School to finance study excursions. The study excursion was immediately recognized as an excellent method for attaining the purposes for which the class was organized.

The objectives of the study excursion as stated by the students in the class, on January 27, just before the start of the trip, indicate that they recognized purposes which are consistent with those of the school and general education. The following is a sample of those objectives in the actual words of the students:

1. To learn about government planning by first-hand evidence.
2. To widen our knowledge of human nature and the kind of life different people lead.
3. To learn of the spirit of co-operation at government projects and to adapt ourselves to this spirit.
4. To learn how to take down impressions in writing, drawing, and photographs.
5. To get an understanding of the tremendous problems in our country.
6. To make a study of regions, their literature, music and culture.
7. To get a better understanding of the people of government works in power, flood control and navigation; to study rural life and learn if possible the reaction of the people toward this new economic planning.
8. To have a good time.
9. To develop new methods of thinking.
10. To study social relationships.
11. To appreciate better all the work that has been done by the TVA. Seeing's believing.
12. To give us a better perspective of national affairs.
13. To get a background of the history and culture of our people.
14. To understand the nation's problems so that we may have attitudes about them.
15. To learn concerning conservation of all national resources—power, soil, etc.
16. To have the experience of living together on a long journey.
17. To enjoy and appreciate our own country.

The following statement of the purposes of the study of national and regional planning, including the preparatory study, the excursion, and the follow-up study, by Miss Elmina R. Lucke, indicates that the staff saw objectives which were more comprehensive than those recognized by the students, but were again in harmony with the aims of general education. From the writer's observations during the study it was evident that in general the staff was in agreement with these purposes.

PURPOSES OF STUDY OF NATIONAL AND REGIONAL PLANNING

I. Book Study—In Preparation

To make students critically intelligent about planning as a crisis in the development of democracy in terms of—
Historical development of government regulation.
Extent of conservation needs and government conservation and other planning projects.
New Deal contributions and complications in planning.
Planning in other countries and societies.

II. Trip to TVA, Sandhills Project, Greenbelt, and Northern Georgia

To strengthen book study of national and regional and community planning by—
Visualization and first-hand experience in large and small aspects of planning.
Opportunity to meet people responsible for such planning and to question them.
Opportunity to learn types of training and social attitudes necessary for such work.
Opportunity to contrast with private industrial planning there, and later, at home.
Opportunity to see concretely good and bad aspects of government.
Opportunity to see housing projects from the inside.
Opportunity to realize the variety of conservation needs.

To see in a little known section of the country—the Southern Highlands—
The beauty of the Great Smokies.
The unique character of the mountain people, the fine racial stock revealed in faces and names, the different standards and philosophies, the evidences of a rich native culture almost lost or forgotten.
The challenge of rural slums.
The effect on people who have moved from undesirable worn-out farms into government jobs and communities.
The effect on professional people (engineers, planning experts, special workers in all fields) who have moved from East or metropolitan centers into the Middle West and possibly Norris.
The status of education and attitudes toward it.

To widen experience by travel, especially to—
Widen horizons geographically and socially.

Train observation to make for alertness.

Develop sympathetic approach to and understanding of individuals and groups who seem on the surface to have nothing in common with New York City young people.

Find more inspiration for aesthetic expression.

To have opportunity to live and work in a local situation in order to—

Feel the joy and satisfaction of living and working close to the soil.

Know farming and village people in their own environment.

Know farming and village people as teachers and guides.

Know and play with young people of their own age who have lived in totally different environment and among different mores.

To feel the hope of the New South and to—

See some of its worst.

Hear planning for its improvement.

Sense its loyalties and its charm.

Enjoy its hospitality.

Hear about the Old South.

Get acquainted with the educated Negro in terms of his problems and needs as well as his music.

Get acquainted with the most gracious aspects of its past through the Williamsburg restoration.

Challenge thought of such developments as Williamsburg in the same cultural setting as the neglected rural area.

III. Thirteen Hundred Miles of Travel by the Whole Senior Class and All Its Teachers—

To learn how to live together with new and mutually respected individual interests and attitudes.

To test friendships and sportsmanship with inconveniences.

To learn how to meet strangers and strange situations with courtesy and respect.

To bring any gifts of our talent to others and to utilize them by bringing home for ourselves impressions of beauty and character and interest.

To break down any of our provincialism of the Atlantic Seaboard.

IV. An Itinerary Which Showed Complete Contrasts in Living Comforts and Conveniences and Opportunities in Order to—

Gain new respect for the too casually accepted gifts of electricity and other magic of the Machine Age.

Begin to appreciate the drama that lies in the harnessing of Power to transform modern civilization.

V. Follow-Up Discussion and Reports and Further Study in Order to—

Build from simple observation and listening to wider and deeper knowledge.

Clarify meanings and back impressions with facts.

Improve knowledge and vocabulary in concepts of social and economic relationships.

See in the large how human living is conditioned by the physical world.

Realize how cultural living is affected by technological changes.

Develop some honest thinking and opinions as to what democracy really means in our society.

Develop some honest thinking and opinions of the place and need of social and economic planning in our own society if it endeavors to retain what democracy it has, and to become more democratic.

Influence the rest of the year's study of Living in Contemporary America with realistic experiences as points of departure.

THE STUDY EXCURSION AS A TECHNIQUE FOR ACHIEVING SOME OF
THE AIMS OF GENERAL EDUCATION

The study excursion may be used as a technique for achieving some of the purposes of general education. General education aims to bring the individual into contact with the culture, thus emphasizing the individual as he functions in a changing society. It aims to develop information, skill, generalizations, application, interests, and appreciations in such a way as maximally to realize the potentialities of the learner in reference to the needs of the society that is and that is to be. Among the values claimed by educators for the study excursion technique are that it makes education practical since it involves the realities of life, affords valuable vocational and educational guidance, and provides opportunity for the development of initiative, leadership, and a sense of responsibility. Initiative, leadership, a sense of responsibility, vocational guidance, and educational guidance are certainly outcomes which, if realized, will contribute to the development of an individual who functions more intelligently in a changing society.

in each experiment—by motion pictures, by study of library references, by a seminar, and by a class demonstration. He found that the study excursion technique was superior to all four variants of the classroom study and discussion technique in the production of gain in knowledge. He lists some "non-statistical results" which he believes study excursions possess. These include the ability to increase interest in school work, the ability to develop attitudes of increased co-operativeness, the ability to unify school and community life, and the ability to clarify principles. It should be noted here that statistical evaluations of some outcomes similar to Grinstead's "non-statistical results" are among the purposes of the present investigation.

THE PROBLEM RESTATED

In view of the possibility that the study excursion may be one valuable technique for implementation of some of the aims of general education, the present investigation was planned to measure certain of the possible outcomes of the Lincoln School senior class study excursion. The outcomes concerning which measurement was attempted are as follows:

1. Growth in understanding of the problems of soil erosion and land management, and growth in understanding of the procedures and processes used to convert energy of falling water into useful electrical energy.

2. Changes in attitude toward the following public problems:
   a. Public relief.
   b. Unlimited individual initiative in farming.
   c. Socio-economic planning.
   d. Conservation.
   e. Private ownership of utilities.

3. Changes in opinions regarding the following propositions:
   a. An individual farmer should possess the sole right to make decisions in regard to the farming practice on his own farm.
   b. It is wise for the government to lead in the development of the kinds of socio-economic planning carried on in the Tennessee Valley.
   c. It is wise for the government to enter the power business in competition with existing private power companies.

d. Communism, civil war, people's fronts, national governments, and central economic planning are all different forms of a revolt against private monopolies.

e. Planning is not something new; it is the very stuff of which civilization has been made.

f. We are sure to have for the next generation an increasing contest between those who have and those who have not.

g. Governments should come to the assistance of people who have low standards of living, even if those people are not enthusiastic about receiving such assistance.

4. Growth in ability to identify evidence of poor land management and procedures for better land management.

5. Growth in ability to recognize the application of principles of land management.

6. Growth in ability to recognize the application of principles of power production.

7. Growth in ability to generalize in regard to land management.

8. Growth in ability to generalize in regard to power production.

9. Evidences of other growths, such as in reflective thinking and in personal relationships.

Specifically, evidence will be sought which may answer the following questions:

1. Does the study excursion result in growths, losses, or changes with respect to the outcomes listed above?

2. What is the relationship between the teachers' opinions of the students' attitudes and the attitudes as shown by objective measurement?

3. What is the relationship between the teachers' estimate of information gains and the gains shown by objective measurement?

4. Are the learning experiences of the study excursion such as to increase interrelatedness among attitudes?

5. Are there changes in relationship between students' information and their ability to generalize and to apply principles?

6. Is there any relationship between gain in information and change in attitude?

7. If the participants in the excursion are divided into three groups according to ability, which group will profit most from the experiences of the excursion?

SUMMARY

Examination of literature relative to the study excursion has shown that it is a technique which may be used by educators to attain some of the purposes of general education. Since little has been done to evaluate the outcomes of study excursions by means of recognized scientific techniques, such an evaluation is needed. Determination of some of the outcomes of a study excursion should assist educators in deciding whether the study excursion is a good method for attaining the purposes of general education. Such determination should also throw light upon the question of the utility of excursions for special forms of education, but that problem is not the concern of this report.

CHAPTER III

PROCEDURES

THE twenty boys and twenty-six girls who participated in the Lincoln School senior class study excursion were the students whose scores on certain instruments of evaluation form the basis for this report. Evaluation of growths in understanding, changes in attitude, changes in opinions, and growths in ability to identify, to recognize the application of principles, and to generalize[1] was effected by means of comparable "before" and "after" tests, anecdotal records kept by the author, and examination of student diaries. It was necessary to develop ways and means to measure the outcomes proposed for evaluation. It is essential to recognize that differences—in the sense of growths, losses, and changes—were the objectives in order to understand that the measurements should be made "before" and "after." Before the preparatory study was begun by the class a battery of tests was administered by the author. After the class returned from the excursion, some tests were again administered and the entire battery was repeated at the end of the follow-up study period. The method of measuring each of these outcomes of the study excursion, under the conditions of study, will be described separately. Where special tests were required, their construction will be outlined.

INFORMATION TEST

The information test used in this study was designed to evaluate growth in understanding of problems of soil erosion and land management and of procedures and processes used to convert energy of falling water into useful electrical energy. As there was no test available which could serve this purpose, the author constructed one using multiple choice questions. The following is a copy of this test.

[1] See Chapter I, pp. 7-8.

27

Information Test

Name.............................. Date...............

Age....................... Date of birth...............

Are you going on the trip to Tennessee Valley?....................?

List the science courses you have taken..........................

Directions: In each of the following groups of items you will find three statements in the right-hand column, each of which characterizes or suggests one of the five items listed opposite in the left-hand column. In the parenthesis following each statement, write the number corresponding to the item in the left-hand column to which it applies or with which it is *most* significantly associated. The items in the left-hand column may be used more than once. The first exercise has been correctly worked out to show you how to proceed.

Sample

1. Dust	0. Dry, finely divided soil....... (1)
2. Rivers	0. Sometimes useful for navigation (2)
3. Clouds	0. May be the habitat of fish..... (2)
4. Rain	
5. Snow	

---

1. Run-off	1. The moisture which is dropped in the form of rain, snow, etc., when moisture-laden air is cooled ( )
2. Absorption	2. Water held by the surface soil.. ( )
3. Precipitation	3. Water surplus penetrates by gravity to the underground strata of the soil .... ( )
4. Infiltration	
5. Water table	

---

1. Contour plowing	Three practices which partly compensate for the removal of vegetative cover and disturbance of soil firmness by farm machinery
2. Draining the ponds	
3. Cultivation during the growing season	4. .... ( )
4. Plowing a straight furrow	5. .... ( )
5. Strip farming	6. .... ( )

---

1. Strip farming
2. Contour plowing
3. Constructing many highways and railroads
4. Washing of the top soil into the streams
5. Restoring swamps

7. Increases amount of run-off.... ( )
8. An irreparable loss of natural resources .... ( )
9. May conflict with good health protection .... ( )

---

1. Rock
2. Clay
3. Humus
4. Silt
5. Vegetative cover

10. Makes soil porous........... ( )
11. Combats silting of reservoirs... ( )
12. Colloidal material which decreases the amount of absorption and infiltration .... ( )

---

1. Spruce
2. Willow
3. Black locust
4. Pine
5. Oak

13. The best tree for controlling badly eroded land........... ( )
14. A legume hence it enriches the soil with nitrate............. ( )
15. Usually grows as a shrub with many branches .... ( )

---

1. Money
2. Over-cropping
3. Natural resources
4. Erosion
5. Wheat

16. The basis of all economic life.. ( )
17. Progress or decadence of a people is determined by the manner in which they use........... ( )
18. Washing away of rich top soils.. ( )

---

1. Waste of a natural resource
2. Balance of land and water
3. Conservation
4. Beaver dams
5. Floods

19. Seriously impaired by the methods of agriculture, grazing, and forest abuse practiced today.... ( )
20. Large proportions of the water precipitated on the land surface find their way to the oceans without having rendered their potential service to man.......... ( )
21. May destroy human lives...... ( )

1. Erosion
2. Corrosion
3. Silting
4. Open listing
5. Strip cropping

22. Reservoirs may become filled with material transported by streams and rivers .... ( )
23. Fields may be plowed in such a manner as to produce alternate strips of hollows and ridges... ( )
24. Washing away of fertile surface soils is an important problem in the Tennessee Valley......... ( )

---

1. Building large dams
2. Building furrows at right angles to the direction of flow
3. Building fences
4. Building furrows up and down the slope
5. Building terraces

25. Method of establishing backwaters and restoring swamps and marshes .... ( )
26. Method which is conducive to erosion .... ( )
27. Method which combats erosion by reducing the rate at which run-off flows .... ( )

---

1. Two feet
2. Ten feet
3. 7,000,000 acre-feet
4. 1,000,000 acre-feet
5. 3,500,000 acre-feet

28. Total storage on the present Tennessee River projects and those recommended .... ( )
29. Part of the total storage of the Tennessee System provided by main-river dams .... ( )
30. Additional freeboard provided for the Mississippi levees by the Tennessee projects .... ( )

---

1. Chickamauga dam
2. Wheeler dam
3. Pickwick Landing dam
4. Hales Bar dam
5. Guntersville dam

31. Dam under construction about 200 miles above the mouth of the Tennessee River .... ( )
32. A completed combined navigation, flood control and hydroelectric project .... ( )
33. Operated by the Tennessee Electric Power Company......... ( )

---

1. Transformers in the power house
2. Pumps
3. Vanes
4. Transformers near the consumer
5. Shaft

34. Receives low voltage, high amperage current and converts it to high voltage, low amperage current .... ( )
35. Used for safety purposes...... ( )
36. Part of a turbine........... ( )

---

1. Spillway
2. Sluice
3. Penstock
4. Lock
5. Head

37. The distance between the level of water supply and the point at which the water leaves the turbine ( )
38. Pipe used to lead water to a turbine .... ( )
39. A device for letting water in or out or holding it back........ ( )

---

1. Kilowatt
2. Ohm
3. Watts
4. Ampere
5. Volt

40. Volts multiplied by amperes *.. ( )
41. Unit for measuring the rate of flow of electricity........... ( )
42. 6.3 times 10^{18} electrons per second .... ( )

---

1. Force
2. Speed
3. Power
4. Work
5. Energy

43. The time rate of doing work... ( )
44. The accomplishment of a force exerted through a distance.... ( )
45. A push or a pull which tends to distort a body or change its condition of rest or motion....... ( )

---

1. Carbon
2. Vanadium
3. Tungsten
4. Lead
5. Iron alloys

46. Filament used in modern incandescent lamps .... ( )
47. Used to make fuses.......... ( )
48. Used to make the cores of armatures .... ( )

---

* This statement refers to direct current.

1. Motor
2. Generator
3. Transformer
4. Rectifier
5. Induction coil

49. A device for converting alternating current to direct current... ( )
50. A device for changing the voltage and amperage of alternating current .... ( )
51. A device for producing electrical pressure by moving conductors continuously through a magnetic field .... ( )

---

1. A kilowatt-hour
2. A cycle
3. A kilowatt
4. A horse power
5. A milli-watt

52. The unit used in rating generators and for most power measurements .... ( )
53. One thousand watts.......... ( )
54. 746 watts .... ( )

---

1. Balanced culture
2. Land-water culture
3. Metal-culture
4. Modern American culture
5. Pure culture

55. Foundation upon which all cultures are built.............. ( )
56. Has seriously disturbed the natural operation of the hydrologic cycle .... ( )
57. The methods of activity of a people are in harmony with the natural relationships of soil, water and living things............ ( )

---

1. Forests and vegetation
2. Bare plowed soil
3. Excessive run-off
4. Too little run-off
5. Evaporation

58. Results when the normal process of providing a store of ground water through absorption and infiltration is not maintained.. ( )
59. Washes away fertile top soils.. ( )
60. Promotes penetration of water to deep storage basins in the ground water region......... ( )

---

1. Plant vegetative cover
2. Use fertilizer
3. Build higher dams
4. Summer fallow
5. Grow corn every year on the same land

61. Method of minimizing the silting of reservoirs............ ( )
62. Method of restoring depleted soil .... ( )
63. Method of robbing the soil.... ( )

1. Increases absorption
2. Grass land
3. Clean-tilled
4. Decreases infiltration
5. Single-crop land

64. Treatment of streams in such a manner as to hasten the flow of unused water to the sea....... ( )
65. A term applied to certain crops which are intensely cultivated.. ( )
66. More susceptible to erosion.... ( )

---

1. Replanted forests
2. Extremely steep hill-sides
3. Cultivated hillsides
4. Level land
5. Natural woodland

67. Should never be cultivated.... ( )
68. Gives amazingly efficient protection against erosion.......... ( )
69. Restoration of eroded land.... ( )

---

1. Corn
2. Clover
3. Wheat
4. Pastures
5. Timber

Three good vegetative covers for land

70. .... ( )
71. .... ( )
72. .... ( )

---

1. Plowing a straight furrow
2. Planting permanent pastures
3. Burning stump and litter after lumbering operations
4. Cutting pine forests
5. Planting wheat

73. A means of conserving soil and water .... ( )
74. A means of destroying humus.. ( )
75. A means of encouraging erosion from run-off .... ( )

---

1. Spillways
2. Restoration of water reservoirs
3. Over-drainage
4. Water table
5. Soil-drifting

76. Causes diminished ground water supply .... ( )
77. May help to increase the ground water supply .... ( )
78. Determines the height at which water will stand in a well...... ( )

1. Contour plowing
2. Strip-farming
3. Terracing
4. Rotating crops
5. Basin listing

79. Especially useful on extremely steep slopes .... ( )
80. Especially useful in regions where periods of extremely heavy rainfall are followed by periods of drought............ ( )
81. A plan which often includes the growth of legumes............ ( )

---

1. One-quarter
2. 1,000,000
3. 2,500,000
4. 40,000
5. One-half

82. Population of Tennessee Valley area .... ( )
83. Drainage area of the Tennessee River in square miles......... ( )
84. Proportion of the Tennessee River Basin which is covered by forests .... ( )

---

1. Watts Bar dam
2. Wilson dam
3. Pickwick Landing dam
4. Wheeler dam
5. Guntersville dam

85. A dam, already constructed, but which is to be raised between one and two feet................ ( )
86. Completed dam, 15½ miles above Wilson dam............ ( )
87. Dam under construction...... ( )

---

1. Series-parallel
2. Tuned
3. Series
4. Shunt
5. Parallel

88. A circuit in which the negative terminal of each part of the circuit is joined to the positive terminal of the next part........ ( )
89. A circuit in which the total resistance is the sum of the resistance of the parts............ ( )
90. The circuit used to connect the lamps in a house............ ( )

---

1. A. C.
2. D. C.
3. Primary current
4. High voltage direct current
5. Induced current

91. Generators use two slip rings instead of a commutator........ ( )
92. Most frequently used in transmission lines .... ( )
93. Produced by an ordinary dry cell ( )

1. 600 watt-hours
2. 200 watt-hours
3. 12 kilowatt-hours
4. 7 kilowatt-hours
5. 40 watt-hours

94. Three kilowatts of power flow-
    ing for four hours........... ( )
95. Five 40-watt lamps burning for
    three hours each............. ( )
96. Two 40-watt heating units burn-
    ing for half an hour.......... ( )

---

1. Chemical
2. Light
3. Heat
4. Sound
5. Kinetic

97. The form of energy to which
    electrical energy is converted and
    lost when it is sent through a
    transmission line .... ( )
98. The two forms of energy to
    which electrical energy is con-
    verted in a lamp............. ( )
    .... ( )

---

1. Circuit-breakers
2. Solenoids
3. Electric motors
4. Electric generators
5. Electromagnets

99. A coil, carrying a current and
    having an iron core.......... ( )
100. Uses electricity to produce mo-
     tion or to do work........... ( )
101. Used to prevent an electric cir-
     cuit from carrying too much cur-
     rent .... ( )

---

1. Voltmeter
2. Galvanometer
3. Ammeter
4. Kilowatt-hour meter
5. Milliammeter

102. Device used to measure differ-
     ences in electrical pressure..... ( )
103. Device used to measure very
     small currents .... ( )
104. Device used to measure quantity
     of energy used by a consumer.. ( )

In constructing the test, books and articles relative to soil erosion, land management, and power production were consulted. Much helpful material was found in a joint publication of the Soil Conservation Service, Resettlement Administration, and Rural Electrification Administration entitled *Little Waters* [19]. From these sources pertinent and important items of information were selected by judgment. This list of information items formed the basis for the construction of five hundred test items of the form shown above. These test items were revised a number of times after criticism. The one hundred four items used in the final test were selected by random sampling of the five hundred.

KELLEY-REMMERS ATTITUDE SCALE [18]

Through examination of the objectives and plans for the study excursion and through consultation with officials of Lincoln School and Teachers College, it was decided that the study excursion might be expected to influence the students' attitudes in regard to the following:

A. Public relief.
B. Unlimited individual initiative in farming.
C. Socio-economic planning.
D. Conservation.
E. Private ownership of utilities.

The instrument chosen as a measure for these attitudes was *A Scale for Measuring Attitude Toward Any Institution* by Kelley and Remmers [18]. The following instructions including definitions of the above issues were given to the students:

In the five spaces at the head of the ruled columns on the front page of the test you will fill in the five phrases I tell you. In the first space you will write the words, "public relief." By "public" we mean the nation as a whole, the state, or the local community. By "relief" we mean aid in the form of money or necessities for indigent persons in return for which the persons do not render service. Thus by "public relief" we mean such aid paid for by the public. Fill in the column now and follow the directions at the head of the test. If the instructions are not clear, ask your questions now.

Time was allowed for reaction to the above; then the instructions continued as follows:

In the second space you will write the words, "unlimited individual initiative in farming." "Unlimited individual initiative" means that the individual possesses the *sole* right to make decisions in regard to farming practice. By farming we mean the use of land for agricultural purposes.

After lapse of sufficient time for reaction to the above, the instructions continued as follows:

In the third space you will write the words, "socio-economic planning." By "socio-economic" we mean having both social and economic aspects; social in reference to people; economic in reference to farming, industry, occupations, trades, professions, etc. By "planning" we mean a scheme of action which considers the effects upon future conditions. Here the term refers to planning by the community, the governments and experts appointed by the governments.

Again sufficient time was allowed for reaction; then the following instructions were given:

In the fourth space you will write the word, "conservation." By "conservation" we mean restoring or protecting the natural resources we have and attempting to restore the natural resources we have wasted.

After another lapse of time for reaction, the final instructions were given as follows:

In the fifth space you will write the words, "private ownership of utilities." By "utilities" we mean enterprises which supply some commodity (gas, electricity, power, water) to the community where the enterprise involves a monopoly or a near monopoly.

Kelley [17 : 18–36] defines "institution" as used in the test to be "anything forming a characteristic and persistent fixture in social and national life" or as "any establishment of public character." She [17 : 26] states that the reliability of the test as indicated by correlation of the two forms varies from .71 to .98 when used for various "institutions."

The validity of the test [17 : 29] was determined by the two general methods of validation: (*a*) by correlation with specific attitude scales as outside criteria; (*b*) by using the test to measure groups whose attitude is known. The correlation coefficients found by the first procedure varied from .83 to .98. Kelley [17 : 33] summarizes the results of the second procedure as follows: "Since we know the attitude of the Catholic Church toward divorce, the expectation would be that members of this church would score very low in attitude toward divorce. The scale showed this."

The test is scaled so that the limits of score variations are from 0.0 to 11.0. A low score indicates opposition to the institution in question and a high score indicates approval of the institution. A score of 6.0–6.9 indicates neutrality. (See reference 18 for type responses.)

OPINIONS TEST

After a preliminary examination of the results of the first application of the Kelley-Remmers scale, the experimenter felt that the necessity of responding only to a list of predetermined statements might prevent the students from revealing their actual attitudes on the issues involved. It was also discovered that the attitudes shown on some issues were already extreme, and thus possibilities for change, as measured by this instrument, were decidedly limited in one direction. For these reasons it was decided to devise another instrument for measurement of attitudes and to include attitudes other than those measured by the Kelley-Remmers scale.

The procedure employed was to select a number of pertinent issues by examination of relevant literature and consultation with informed individuals. Spontaneous opinions upon these issues were obtained from the students on January 27, 1938, by means of the following "test" (referred to as the Opinions Test):

Opinions Test

Name...............

What is your opinion in regard to each of the following statements? You may agree, disagree, or take any intermediate position, but briefly state your *reasons*.

1. An individual farmer should possess the sole right to make decisions in regard to the farming practice on his own farm.
2. It is wise for the government to lead in the development of the kinds of socio-economic planning carried on in the Tennessee Valley.
3. It is wise for the government to enter the power business in competition with existing private power companies.
4. Communism, civil war, people's fronts, national governments and central economic planning are all different forms of a revolt against private monopolies.
5. Planning is not something new; it is the very stuff of which civilization has been made.

6. We are sure to have for the next generation an increasing contest between those who have and those who have not.

7. Governments should come to the assistance of people who have low standards of living, even if those people are not enthusiastic about receiving such assistance.

On February 14, shortly after the class returned from the South, the same "test" was repeated.

Measurement of these spontaneous opinions was attempted by the process of serial or order-of-merit arrangement of the statements—a process usually called ranking.[2] Each opinion given by each student was typed on a separate card and the card keyed with a number which indicated the name of the student, the issue to which it was a reaction and whether it was offered before or after the excursion; e.g., 43060 on a card indicated that the opinion was a reaction to issue 4, offered by student number 30 (E. H.) on the second testing. (Even numbers indicated second testing; odd numbers indicated first testing.) These numbers were meaningless without the key. All the cards with opinions on issue 1 were placed in a pile. Similarly the cards for issues 2, 3, 4, 5, 6, and 7 were placed in separate piles. Each pile contained both the "before" and the "after" opinions on a single issue. Competent judges, including professors of Teachers College and students in the Advanced School of Education of Teachers College, were asked to rank these in accordance with the following instructions:

There are approximately 90 opinions about the above issue (each set of instructions contained a statement of the appropriate issue). You are being asked to judge the opinions on this issue. Please arrange the cards so that they are ranked from those which express the most thorough agreement with the statement of the issue to those which express the most thorough disagreement. When you have finished place them in a pile so that according to your judgment the top card expresses the most agreement, the bottom card the most disagreement, and the intervening ones are arranged in order of agreement.

Three judges were asked to rank the opinions on each issue. The cards were thoroughly shuffled before being given to each judge.

[2] Hull [15 : 382–390] describes the method completely.

Every time the cards were returned to the experimenter, a record was made by typing the key numbers in the order in which they were placed.

When the three judges had arranged the cards for a given issue, the ranks assigned were transferred to each card, with a letter to indicate the name of the judge who assigned the rank. The rank positions were converted to per cent positions by using the technique described by Hull [15 : 388].[3] These per cent positions in the ranked series were then converted into scores or units of amount on an ordinary scale of one hundred points as described by Hull [15 : 387]. Card number 61530 shown below illustrates the appearance of each card after this process.[4]

61530
Yes. The contest between those who have
and those who have not has been increasing
and is increasing now.

	H.	Ha.	F.
R.	8	15	19.5
P.	9.1	17.6	23.2
T.	76	68	65

Average = 70

The rank of 19.5 results from the fact that two opinions which would have been assigned ranks of 19 and 20 respectively were judged equal and hence assigned the average rank. The score assigned to each opinion was the average of the scores computed from the rankings of the three judges. A high score indicated agreement with the statement of the issue and a low score indicated disagree-

[3] Per cent position = $\dfrac{100\,(R - .5)}{N}$ where R means the assigned rank and N means the number of cards.

[4] H., Ha., and F. refer to the three judges, Howard, F. T., Hartmann, (Prof.) G. W., and Fraser, James A.
R. means the ranks assigned to this opinion by each of the three judges.
P. is the computed per cent position.
T. is the scale score.

ment. This corresponds with the interpretation of the Kelley-Remmers scores.

An index to the reliability of the rankings and resultant scores was obtained by correlating the judges' scores resulting from the three rankings. These correlations are summarized in Table I. The validity of using the average of the scores given by the three judges is indicated best by the average inter-r. In issue number 2 application of the Spearman-Brown formula shows that if three equally good repetitions of judgment are combined they would correlate with the combined scores of three other equally good repetitions to the extent of .82. This correlation is sufficiently high to warrant the use of the average scores to indicate group trends. The measures for each individual are not assumed to be reliable. All other average inter-r's are higher, and thus will yield higher reliability coefficients. Therefore all of the average scores may be used to indicate group trends.

The final step necessary to obtain distributions of comparable "before" and "after" scores on each issue was to separate the cards with even key numbers from those with odd key numbers.

This measure of attitude or opinion trends serves as a partial check on the Kelley-Remmers scale as issues 1, 2, 3, and 7 are similar to those measured by that instrument.

TABLE I

INTERCORRELATIONS AMONG THREE JUDGES * CONCERNING THE RANK OF OPINIONS BY ISSUES

	Issue 1	Issue 2	Issue 3	Issue 4	Issue 5	Issue 6	Issue 7
r12................	.90	.56	.91	.68	.87	.66	.75
r13................	.81	.65	.85	.74	.92	.71	.74
r23................	.90	.59	.78	.83	.97	.71	.88
Average inter-r†	.876	.601	.855	.757	.932	.694	.800

* Judges 1, 2, and 3 are not the same judges for each issue.
† The average inter-r was found by converting the correlation coefficients to Fisher's Z correlation function, adding, dividing by 3 and converting back to r.

LAND MANAGEMENT IDENTIFICATION TEST

The Land Management Identification Test was planned to measure growth in ability to identify evidences of poor land management and procedures for better land management. Slides for projection by a lantern were made from the diagrams (Diagrams 1 and 2) of the Report of the Great Plains Committee [12 : 17–19]. Capital letters were placed on the slides so that when projected various features could be identified by letter. This test was combined with a Land Management Principles Test and a Land Management Generalizations Test. All three are shown below.

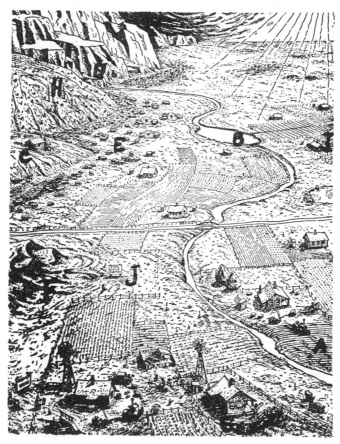

DIAGRAM 1

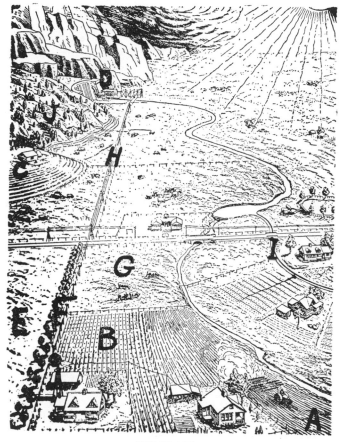

DIAGRAM 2

Name............................. Date....................

On the screen you will be shown two diagrams with letters placed in various parts. Below is a list of ten terms. The first four refer to Diagram 1; the next six to Diagram 2. After each term, place the appropriate letter or letters of the diagram.

1. Rill and gully erosion
2. Over-grazing
3. Wind erosion
4. Check dam
5. Power dam

6. Terraces
7. Contour plowing
8. Strip farming
9. Wind break
10. Power distribution

Some Principles of Land Management

1. Denudation of the more accessible timberlands results in an increase in run-off.
2. Disturbance of the natural vegetative cover removes the protection from the soil.
3. Drainage of swamps results in a lowering of the water table.
4. From the point of view of making productive land available, drainage is beneficial.
5. Transpiration and evaporation have a considerable influence on cloud formation and rainfall.
6. Over-grazing destroys the young sprouts and grass.
7. When litter and humus are destroyed, the soils they have protected and kept open are exposed to the mechanical influence of falling and running water.
8. The force of increased run-off washes the soils into the ponds and streams.
9. Clean-tilled land is susceptible to erosion.
10. Single-crop land is susceptible to erosion.
11. Water should render its potential service to man before finding its way to the ocean.
12. Land should be cultivated in such a manner as to decrease the rate of run-off.
13. Wind-swept land should not be broken.
14. The per acre productivity of land declines as the elements for plant life are leached out.
15. Physical factors have no regard for line fences between farms.
16. Grasses and herbs contribute to the humus, increase the supply of water for irrigation.
17. Retardation of the flow of surface water increases the supply of water for irrigation.
18. Plans which create reservoirs increase the supply of ground water.
19. Submarginal land should be devoted to vegetative cover.
20. Reservoirs of water should be created.
21. Erosion control facilitates the regulation of headwaters of streams.
22. Extremely steep slopes should be replanted in forests.
23. Controlled grazing is more profitable from the long-time viewpoint.
24. The slope of moderately sloping cultivated land should be decreased whenever possible.
25. Waters should be made to flow as slowly as possible.

In Diagram 1, which of the above principles are illustrated at:

A.	F. ....
B.	G. ....
C.	H. ....
D.	I. ....
E.	J. ....

In Diagram 2, which of the above principles are illustrated at:

A.	F. ....
B.	G. ....
C.	H. ....
D.	I. ....
E.	J. ....

In Diagram 1, what generalizations concerning the management and inter-relationship of soil, water, and living things can you draw from each of the following:

A.	F.
B.	G.
C.	H.
D.	I.
E.	J.

In Diagram 2, what generalizations concerning the management and inter-relationship of soil, water, and living things can you draw from each of the following:

A.	F.
B.	G.
C.	H.
D.	I.
E.	J.

A scoring key was developed by submitting the test to three experts:[5] Professor Paul B. Sears, Professor O. S. Morgan, and James A. Fraser. These three, after taking the test independently, agreed on all answers and they were accepted as correct. Five points were allowed for each correct identification.

[5] The use of experts for the determination of scoring keys is characteristic of this study. Such experts were chosen primarily because of their wide reputation for competence in the area of knowledge needed to answer the test. In addition their availability for, and willingness to do, the work influenced the final choice. Because of intensive study preparatory to constructing the tests, the author, when necessary, considered himself an expert.

LAND MANAGEMENT PRINCIPLES TEST

The Land Management Principles Test is shown combined with the Land Management Identification Test. It uses the list of twenty-five principles of land management.

The scoring key was developed by submitting the test to six experts: Professors Paul B. Sears, George T. Renner, Jr., O. S. Morgan, Edmund deS. Brunner, and John E. Orchard, and James A. Fraser. Each expert took the test independently, with the following instructions:

> Please answer the part pertaining to principles of land management. Note that correct answers are those that *illustrate* the principles.

Since the experts did not agree[6] completely on the answers, a key was prepared based on the number of experts who did agree that a given principle was illustrated at a given location. For example, at location B on Diagram 1 the experts enumerated the following principles:

Experts	Number of Principle in the List 1 2 3 4 5 6 7 8 9 10 11 12 13 14 15 16 17 18 19 20 21 22 23 24 25
Sears.........	x x x x
Renner.......	x x x x
Fraser........	x x x
Morgan......	x x x x x x
Brunner......	
Orchard......	x x x
Number who agreed......	1 2 2 2 3 5 5
Score to be given student for enumerating	$\frac{1}{2}$ 1 1 1 $1\frac{1}{2}$ $2\frac{1}{2}$ $2\frac{1}{2}$

[6] Since decision as to whether a given principle is illustrated at a given location in the diagram must be based upon knowledge of the relationships involved and upon human judgment, the use of experts to determine the scoring key becomes particularly pertinent. It is the element of human judgment in the decision which explains disagreement among experts.

A score of ten was allotted to each location. This was divided among the acceptable answers, approximately in proportion to the number of experts who agreed on each answer. In the above example, twenty answers were submitted by all the judges. A score of 1 out of the 20 was given to principle number 5, so the score of a student who gave only answer number 5 would be (1/20 of 10) = ½. Similarly, principle 25 is valued at (5/20 of 10) = 2½. A student can obtain a perfect score only by checking all the answers that were checked by the experts. His score on the whole test will be the sum of the scores obtained thus for each of the twenty locations.

LAND MANAGEMENT GENERALIZATIONS TEST

The Land Management Generalizations Test also is shown with the Land Management Identification Test. Evaluation of these generalizations was effected by the ranking technique previously described. Each generalization was typed on a separate card and keyed so that the date of the test, the location, the diagram, and the individual could be identified. Three science students of the Advanced School of Education [7] were asked to rank the cards in order from those which they considered good generalizations to those which

TABLE II

INTERCORRELATIONS AMONG THREE JUDGES * CONCERNING THE RANK OF GENERALIZATIONS ON LAND MANAGEMENT GENERALIZATIONS TEST, BY LOCATIONS †

	1A	1B	1C	1D	1E	1F	1G	1H	1I	2A	2B	2C	2D	2E	2F	2G	2H	2I
r12......	.86	.75	.93	.92	.78	.74	.88	.95	.77	.66	.92	.83	.96	.89	.82	.65	.87	.71
r13......	.70	.73	.89	.78	.92	.90	.83	.89	.49	.90	.86	.79	.77	.81	.87	.84	.81	.77
r23......	.75	.59	.78	.77	.72	.81	.95	.85	.82	.62	.88	.67	.79	.85	.86	.85	.90	.86
Average inter-r.	.78	.70	.88	.81	.83	.83	.90	.91	.72	.76	.89	.77	.87	.85	.85	.79	.86	.77

* Judges 1, 2, and 3 are the same judges for each location.
† Location 1A means location on Diagram 1. Other locations are interpreted similarly.
[7] The author acted as one of these students. The other two were graduate students in science education, and had had considerable experience with the problems of land management.

they considered poor. The technique described by Hull [15 : 382–390] was employed to convert these ranks to scores. Reliability of the ranking is indicated by the coefficients of correlation between scores as derived from the three separate rankings, shown in Table II. These indexes indicate that the three independent rankers are sufficiently in agreement to warrant use of the mean scores.

Upon examination of the poor generalizations it was discovered that those which had received scores below 40 were not generalizations at all. Most of them were mere identification of the indicated part of the diagram. To penalize for failure to generalize, the following conversion key was used to convert the scores to new ones:

Score	New Score
90–99.9	6
80–89.9	5
70–79.9	4
60–69.9	3
50–59.9	2
40–49.9	1
00–39.9	0

POWER PRINCIPLES TEST

The purpose of the Power Principles Test was to evaluate growth in ability to recognize the application of principles of power production. A diagram of penstock, turbine, turbine shaft, generator, and tail water was mimeographed. Each portion was indicated by letters from A to E. Below the diagram (Diagram 3) was a list of twelve numbered principles. The students were asked to indicate the numbers of the principles illustrated at each lettered location.

Principles

1. The energy of falling water is converted into energy of turning vanes.
2. Falling water is controlled so that its energy may be conveniently used.
3. Potential energy may be converted into kinetic energy.
4. Kinetic energy may be converted into potential energy.
5. Energy of mechanical motion may be converted into electrical energy.

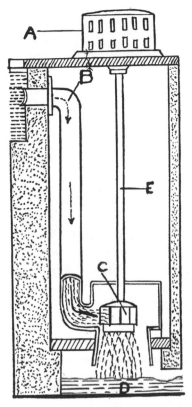

DIAGRAM 3

6. A coil of wire, rotating in a magnetic field is used to convert energy from one form to another.
7. The value of water in producing power depends upon the distance it falls.
8. When water cannot fall, it is not useful for the purposes of power production.
9. Electrical energy can be converted into other forms of energy.
10. The lifting force of a fluid is equal to the difference between the weight of the object and the weight of the same volume of the fluid displaced.
11. For every action there is an equal and opposite reaction.
12. The pressure exerted by water is directly dependent upon the depth.

Which of the above principles are applied at:

A. .... D. ....
B. .... E. ....
C. ....

What generalizations can you make concerning the following parts of the device shown in the diagrams?

A.   D.
B.   E.
C.

Determination of the scoring key was effected by submitting the test to ten experts as follows: Professors Robert von Nardroff, F. W. Hehre, W. I. Slichter, J. W. Russell, G. W. De Harness, Herbert J. Arnold, Harold W. Webb, Dr. H. Emmett Brown, Mr. Warren W. McSpadden, and Mr. W. Lyle Brewer. Since the experts did not completely agree, the values to be allotted were computed by allowing twenty points per location and dividing these among the twelve possible responses in proportion to the number of experts who gave each response. The procedure is described more fully under the heading of "Land Management Principles Test."

POWER GENERALIZATIONS TEST

The Power Generalizations Test is similar in purpose to the Land Management Generalizations Test. It was planned to evaluate the growth in ability to generalize in regard to power production. The portion of the test shown above, which requests the students to make generalizations, was used for this purpose.

Evaluation of these generalizations was effected by the ranking technique previously described. Each generalization, including both the ones made "before" and those made "after," was typed on a card and keyed. Three science students of the Advanced School of Education independently ranked them from those they considered best to those they considered poorest. The technique described by Hull [15 : 382–390] was employed to convert these ranks to scores. Validity of using the average of the three scores is indicated by the coefficients of correlation between scores as derived from the three separate rankings, as shown in Table III. These indexes are sufficiently high to warrant use of the scores.

TABLE III

INTERCORRELATIONS AMONG THREE JUDGES * CONCERNING THE RANK OF GENERALIZATIONS ON POWER GENERALIZATIONS TEST, BY LOCATIONS

	A	B	C	D	E
r_{12}..................	.78	.94	.75	.74	.85
r_{13}..................	.60	.79	.77	.75	.80
r_{23}..................	.73	.68	.63	.69	.88
Average inter-r.......	.71	.84	.72	.73	.85

* Judges 1, 2, and 3 are the same judges for each location.

The mean of the three separate scores was the final score assigned to a given generalization. However, as with the land management generalizations, it was discovered that the scores below 40 represented identification rather than generalization, so the conversion key on page 48 was used to penalize for failure to generalize.

DIARIES

Before leaving New York City, the students were instructed to keep records of their personal reactions to the sights they saw. They were asked to make the record an examination of their own feelings as they traveled and met new experiences. After the excursion these diaries were collected by the author and an attempt was made to grade them. The attempt was abandoned as it seemed profitless in view of the wide variation in both style and content. Instead, each diary was read carefully, and selections were made of parts which indicated reactions to the excursion. The following headings were used as guides in seeking suitable excerpts: evidence of attitudes toward social issues, evidence of critical or reflective thinking, evidence of interest or lack of interest in science, evidence of appreciation or lack of appreciation of scientific achievement. Some of these excerpts are cited in Chapter IV.

TEACHERS' RATING SCALE

An attempt to establish the relationship between the teachers' opinions of the students' attitudes toward the five issues tested by the Kelley-Remmers scale and the students' attitudes as shown by objective measurement was made. A scale containing the definitions of public relief, unlimited individual initiative in farming, socio-economic planning, conservation and private ownership of utilities, previously cited, was constructed. The teachers were asked to rate as many pupils as they felt competent to judge as to their attitude on each of the issues. The following key was used:

    1 means strongly in favor
    2 means mildly in favor
    3 means neutral
    4 means mildly opposed
    5 means strongly opposed

It was the author's plan to have this rating done "before" and "after." Unfortunately, in the rush of getting baggage collected, making last minute plans, and avoiding newspaper reporters and cameramen, most of the teachers did not get an opportunity to give a "before" judgment. However, the subjective judgment of the teachers was solicited after the study excursion; by asking them to rank the students in order of those who changed most to least in acquisition of information during the study excursion. These results are reported in Chapter IV.

SUMMARY

Procedures used in constructing, tabulating, and scoring "before" and "after" tests have been described in this chapter. The information test was a multiple choice type containing 104 items and sampling information from the fields of power production and land management.

The Kelley-Remmers Attitude Scale [18] was used with five issues. An Opinions Test, designed both as a check and as an amplification of the Kelley-Remmers test, has been described. Scoring procedures were based on the technique described by Hull [15 : 382–390].

A test for ability to identify evidences of poor land management and procedures for better management has been described. Correct answers for scoring purposes were determined by pooling the judgment of three experts.

The Land Management Principles Test was designed to evaluate growth in ability to recognize the application of principles of land management. Scoring depended upon distributing credit in proportion to the number of experts who agreed that a given answer was correct.

An adaptation of the technique described by Hull [15 : 382–390] was used to evaluate the generalizations made by students in response to the Land Management Generalizations Test. Use of this technique for this purpose has not previously been made (at least the writer cannot discover a precedent).

The Power Principles Test designed to evaluate growth in ability to recognize the application of principles of power production has been described, together with the method of weighting the scoring in proportion to the number of experts who agreed that an answer was correct.

In the Land Management Generalizations Test and the Power Generalizations Test and the Opinions Test, correlations between the scores determined from judgments of independent rankers are offered as an index to the validity of using the average score given by the three rankers.

CHAPTER IV

ACHIEVEMENT INDICATED BY ANALYSIS OF "BEFORE" AND "AFTER" TESTS

RELATION OF MEASUREMENT PROGRAM TO CHRONOLOGY OF THE EXCURSION

THE measurement program involved a series of "before" and "after" tests. The following is a summary of the relation of this program to the chronology of the excursion:

			Tests Administered
Jan.	3	Preparatory Study begun	Form A, Kelley-Remmers Attitude Scale
Jan.	4		Information Test
Jan.	6		Land Management Identification, Principles, and Generalizations Tests
Jan.	7		Power Principles and Power Generalizations Tests
Jan.	27		Opinions Test
Jan.	28	Preparatory Study ended Excursion begun	
Feb.	8	Excursion ended	
Feb.	9	Follow-up Study started	
Feb.	10		Form B, Kelley-Remmers Attitude Scale
Feb.	14		Opinions Test
Mar.	16	Follow-up Study ended	Information Test and Teachers' Rating
Mar.	28		Land Management Identification, Principles, and Generalizations Tests
Mar.	29		Form A, Kelley-Remmers Attitude Scale and Power Principles and Generalizations Tests

Justification for using on March 16 the same information test used on March 4 was obtained by the following procedure: A list of nine sets of three test items was compiled. It consisted of four sets chosen at random from the test administered on January 4, and five sets chosen at random from the 396 items originally constructed but not used. These questions were given to the class with the following instructions on March 16:

> Some of the following questions were given to you as a pre-test before we went to the South. Please check those which you remember having tried before.

The papers were scored by assigning one credit for each checked set which was on the original test, and one credit for each unchecked set which was not on the original test.

There are nine questions which can be answered either correctly or incorrectly. Assuming chance to be operating exclusively, the average number of questions answered correctly will be 4.5. If chance is assumed, the hypothetical standard deviation will be 1.5.[1] Forty-three students responded to this test, therefore the hypothetical standard deviation of the mean will be 0.2288.[2] The obtained mean was 4.9. The difference between it and the hypothetical mean assuming chance is only 0.4. Application of the test[3] [24 : 365–366] indicates that this small difference is not significantly different from zero.

In the light of this evidence, it seems reasonable to claim that the students had not remembered the test items, and that repetition of the identical information test was justified.

Examination of Table IV reveals that the changes which may be described as reliable in the sense defined are a marked gain in information, a change in the group's attitudes toward unlimited individual initiative in farming, socio-economic planning, and private ownership of utilities, a change in opinion with reference to the proposition that an individual farmer should possess the sole right to make deci-

[1] $\sigma = (kpq)^{1/2} = \sqrt{9(0.5)(0.5)} = \sqrt{2.25} = 1.5.$

[2] $\sigma_M = \dfrac{\sigma}{\sqrt{N}} = \dfrac{1.5}{6.557} = 0.2288.$

[3] $\dfrac{4.9 - 4.5}{0.23} = 1.75.$

TABLE IV—SUMMARY OF MEASUREMENTS *

Measurement Instrument	Mean before Excursion a	Mean after Excursion b	Mean after Follow-up Study c	Diff. $a-b$	Diff. $a-c$	Diff. $b-c$	Mean Diff. σ_{a-b}	Mean Diff. σ_{a-c}	Mean Diff. σ_{b-c}	C.R. $a-b$†	C.R. $a-c$	C.R. $b-c$	r_{ab}	r_{ac}	r_{bc}
Information	33.12		62.76		29.64			1.83			16.16			.53	
Kelley-Remmers Public Relief	7.62	7.41	7.71	-.21	+.09	.30	.33	.21	.31	.64	.41	.96	.62	.78	.68
Kelley-Remmers Unlimited Individual Initiative in Farming	7.01	6.65	5.58	-.36	-1.43	-1.07	.43	.47	.33	.82	3.07	3.26	.50	.42	.67
Kelley-Remmers Socio-economic Planning	9.20	9.71	9.54	.51	.34	-.17	.19	.14	.05	2.76	2.56	3.30	.07	.61	1.00
Kelley-Remmers Conservation	9.49	9.82	9.70	.33	.21	-.12	.14	.14	.08	2.31	1.52	1.48	.31	.42	.29
Kelley-Remmers Private Ownership of Utilities	4.50	6.03	5.71	1.53	1.21	-0.32	.29	.33	.26	5.33	3.66	1.22	.71	.71	.81
Opinions Test Issue 1	53.42	43.67		-9.75			2.39			4.08					
Opinions Test Issue 2	48.17	50.00		1.83			2.57			.71					
Opinions Test Issue 3	52.82	48.53		-4.30			2.44			1.76					
Opinions Test Issue 4	53.03	51.00		-2.03			3.33			.61					
Opinions Test Issue 5	47.91	54.46		6.55			3.77			1.74					
Opinions Test Issue 6	51.65	48.62		-3.03			1.93			1.57					
Opinions Test Issue 7	47.71	53.49		5.77			2.75			2.10					
Land Management Identification	32.91		40.94		8.03			1.95			4.12				
Land Management Principles	18.94		48.80		29.86			8.94			3.34				
Land Management Generalizations	5.09		16.89		11.80			2.11			5.58				
Power Principles	23.30		41.70		18.40			3.79			4.86				
Power Generalizations	2.44		6.88		4.44			1.28			3.48				

* σ mean difference $= \left(\dfrac{s_1^2 - 2r_{12}s_1s_2 + s_2^2}{N-1} \right)^{\frac{1}{2}}$

where s_1 means the standard deviation of the "before" scores and s_2 means the standard deviation of the "after" scores. When the correlation was not computed, the following formula was used:

σ mean difference $= \left(\dfrac{\dfrac{\Sigma(x_1 - x_2)^2}{N} - M_{x_1}^2 - x_2}{N-1} \right)^{\frac{1}{2}}$

† In this chapter the word "reliable" when applied to differences or gains is used in its statistical sense. The critical ratio, which is the ratio of a difference to its standard error, is determined. If the critical ratio is 3 or more, the differences are described in this chapter as "reliable" or "statistically significant." C. R. means critical ratio.

sions in regard to the farming practice on his own farm, a gain in ability to identify evidence of poor land management and procedures for better land management, a gain in ability to recognize the application of principles of land management, a gain in ability to generalize in regard to land management, a gain in ability to recognize the application of principles of power production and a gain in ability to generalize in regard to power production.

In general, this evidence supports the thesis that the study excursion is one procedure for implementation of the philosophy of general education. The changes in attitudes and opinions indicate that information about subject matter and skill in manipulation of subject matter were not glorified as the only or primary outcomes of the excursion. There is ample evidence to show that the students developed ability to generalize from their experiences, and there is adequate evidence to support the claim that they developed ability to recognize the application of information and principles. The gain in information about socially important issues is another important outcome which is consistent with the aim of general education.

The significance of each of the changes, or absence of change, in the various measurements, will be argued separately.

INFORMATION TEST

The study excursion proved to be such that the group showed marked gains in information as measured by this test. The mean score of the "before" test, using only those cases for which both "before" and "after" scores were available, was 33.12, while the mean score of the "after" test was 62.76. The mean gain was thus 29.64. The critical ratio of the mean gain to the standard error of the mean gain was 16.16, indicating that the gain was very reliable. (Table V.)

TABLE V
Information Tests I and II

M Test I	M Test II	S. D. Test I	S. D. Test II	$M_2 - M_1$	C. R.	r_{12}
33.12	62.76	11.24	12.92	29.64	16.16	.53

It is illuminating to compare diary extracts with individual gains. Student number 37, a girl, intensely interested in art and with outstanding ability in art, describes her visit to the powerhouse at Norris Dam as follows:

The powerhouse of Norris Dam is equally beautiful in its simplicity to the shapes of the dam. There, again dominates the architectural simplicity of design, everything being fundamental. There is no factor which would disturb this cold beauty of the miracle of modern era. Even the engineers and mechanics, quietly moving in the halls of the powerhouse, are square-faced, harmonizing perfectly with their surroundings.

One would not expect a girl, exclusively preoccupied by the artistic aspects of her experiences, to show much gain on the information test. This expectation is realized when her "before" and "after" scores reveal a gain of only 13 points—less than half the mean gain for the class. The same experience, a visit to Norris Dam and powerhouse, evokes the following reaction from student number 12, a boy:

The dam proper is built into limestone with a modified type of cement, differing from ordinary Portland cement in the fact that no cooling system such as the one in Boulder Dam was necessary. This is also due to the fact that the dam is about half the bottom thickness of Boulder. It is proof against earthquakes. Strangely enough, there has been no provision made for the silting of the river which the engineer said would fill the lake so as to incapacitate the generators within a hundred fifty years. The pressure against the dam at two hundred feet below the surface of the lake is nearly two hundred pounds per square inch.

The interests of this boy are such that one would expect large gains on the information test. His gain was 34 points. Here is some further evidence for the oft-repeated claim that achievement is closely related to interests.

The diaries cannot be accepted as completely reliable. This is indicated by student 32, a girl whose diary is very superficial and shallow but who shows a gain of 55 points on the information test.

Some estimate of the caliber of the group, their interest and enthusiasm, may be made from the following incident, recorded in the author's personal diary:

The girls were shown the turbines at Norris before the boys. Explanations were made by the usual guide, who was not an engineer. When the girls began to cross-question him, the chief engineer had to be called and when the boys came through, the chief engineer replaced the guide entirely. The engineer-in-charge stated that the group was very much better prepared than most groups who went through his plant.

KELLEY-REMMERS ATTITUDE SCALE

Attitudes toward the five issues measured by this test may be considered as five separate tests. The group's attitude toward public relief is shown by the means of the three applications of the test to be 7.62, 7.41, and 7.71. This indicates mild approval of the institution as defined. The critical ratios of the differences to the standard error of the differences indicate that the changes in attitude are not statistically significant. The relatively high positive correlations among the scores obtained on the three applications of the test indicate that most individuals held steadily to the attitude they had before the study excursion. (For details, see Table VI. All statistics have been computed by using only cases for which three scores are available.) Examination of individual scores shows that a few individuals changed quite radically.

Student Number	First Score	Second Score	Third Score
1	7.1	3.0	6.2
10	6.1	8.9	9.7
27	8.2	3.6	6.1
29	7.6	6.6	10.1
37	8.8	3.9	7.6

Examination of the diaries of these students for evidence on the reason for these changes is not rewarding. Number 37 says, "It is nice to be poor, if you can live in Georgia, and if there is a blue sky with sun." This statement was written during the time her attitude toward public relief was changing from favorable to unfavorable. Perhaps it is significant.

The attitude of the group toward unlimited individual initiative in farming is shown by the means to change progressively in the direction of becoming less favorable to the institution as defined. The change during the time intervening between the first test and the sec-

TABLE VI
SUMMARY OF THE KELLEY-REMMERS ATTITUDE RESULTS

	First Score	Second Score	Third Score	M_2-M_1	C.R.	M_3-M_1	C.R.	M_3-M_2	C.R.	r_{12}	r_{23}	r_{13}
Public relief:												
Mean....	7.62	7.41	7.71	−.21	.64	.09	.41	.30	.96	.62	.68	.78
S. D.....	1.79	2.58	2.08									
Unlimited individual initiative in farming:												
Mean....	7.01	6.65	5.58	−.36	.82	−1.43	3.07	−1.07	3.26	.50	.67	.42
S. D.....	2.72	2.41	2.53									
Socio-economic planning:												
Mean....	9.20	9.71	9.54	.51	2.76	.34	2.56	−.17	3.30	.07	.00	.61
S. D.....	1.04	.58	.82									
Conservation:												
Mean....	9.49	9.82	9.70	.33	2.31	.21	1.52	−.12	1.48	.31	.29	.42
S. D.....	.91	.37	.47									
Private ownership of utilities:												
Mean....	4.50	6.03	5.71	1.53	5.33	1.21	3.66	−0.32	1.22	.71	.81	.67
S. D.....	2.14	2.41	2.66									

Subscripts 1, 2, and 3 refer to tests 1, 2, and 3 respectively. The formula used for r was

$$r_{xy} = \frac{S_x^2 + S_y^2 - S_{x-y}^2}{2S_x S_y}$$

ond is not statistically significant. The critical ratio is only 0.82. The change occurring between test 1 and test 3 is reliable; so, too, is the change between test 2 and test 3. This indicates that the students became less favorable to unlimited individual initiative in farming during the follow-up study period. The reason for this change probably lies in the fact that information and experiences gained during the trip were so abundant that a period of reflection was necessary before they influenced expressed attitudes.

Examination of the individual scores reveals very few changes in a direction opposite to that of the mean change. Student number 23 changed from 4.4 to 5.1 to 7.3. Student number 39 changed from 8.2 to 9.9 to 10.0.

Student number 19 shows scores of 3.4, 4.4, and 3.4. His diary includes a paragraph which illuminates and explains his consistent attitude of opposition to unlimited individual initiative in farming:

Jock Whorley, incidentally, is as we said before, a squatter, different from a Georgia Cracker. His house, before we fixed it, was dilapidated, leaning on one side, with not much roof left. These conditions were fixed up during the morning and mid-afternoon, but nothing can fix up Jock Whorley, or his indigent family. There are many, many children between eight and twelve, plus of course Jock and his wife. He is a lanky fellow, unshaven and lazy to the point of negligence. During our whole two days' work, he does nothing more ambitious than to split about fifty roof shingles. This entails the operation of lifting a blade, resting it on a shingle, and bringing down a weight, times fifty. It is not that he feels inferior, stubborn or resentful. He is just so accustomed to idleness, poverty and misery that he can't get under way. This is one striking example of Dr. Mitchell's oft-repeated words, "Poor land makes poor people, and poor people make poor land." Here is a man who has been so affected by this morale destroying environment that he and his family are being caught in a whirlpool of degradation in a plentiful nation. With absolutely no capital, no reserve, no crop, few clothes, little food and a miserable home, these people typify the problem that must be faced in considering the agricultural aspects of Social Planning. There are a million Jock Whorleys, right now, perched on a stump, with a faraway look in their eyes, and nothing in their minds but dark despair.

The group attitude toward socio-economic planning is shown by the three means—9.20, 9.71, and 9.54. Upon casual examination it would appear that the group became more in favor of socio-economic planning during the pre-study and excursion, and slightly less in favor of it during the follow-up study. Comparison of mean changes with critical ratios reveals that neither the change during the preparatory study and excursion nor the change over the whole period of study is reliable. The only reliable change is the one during the follow-up study and it is very small. Examination of the raw scores reveals that nearly all the students changed very slightly during the latter time, in the direction indicated by the means. It appears to the author that the most reasonable interpretation of these data is that the group were strongly in favor of socio-economic planning as defined, and remained so. The small standard deviations indicate unanimity of opinion. Student number 8 shows this rather interesting series of scores: 5.7, 9.5, 9.7. His diary fails to reveal any interpretive or corroborative evidence.

The group's attitude toward conservation remained consistently favorable throughout. The means are 9.49, 9.82, and 9.70; the critical ratios indicate that none of the changes are significant. Student number 6 writes the following:

> One great problem in the Tennessee Valley is that in winter the cropless fields do not freeze and thus the nitrates are washed out of the soil.

The attitude toward private ownership of utilities shows some interesting changes. The first mean score was 4.50, indicating mild opposition to private ownership. The second mean was 6.03. The change during the preparatory study and excursion was 1.54. It is in the direction of lessened opposition to private ownership. The critical ratio is 5.33, indicating that the change is reliable. The third mean is 5.71, indicating a slight change in the opposite direction or a partial return to the original opposition to private ownership. However, the critical ratio shows that this change is not reliable. The change during the entire study excursion is reliable and indicates lessened opposition to private ownership of utilities. Large standard deviations indicate a wide spread in opinion, which was corroborated by the author's observation of many heated arguments among students concerning this question. Student number 17 shows the following series of scores: 3.0, 2.7, and 3.2. These indicate strong and unrelenting opposition to private ownership. His diary contains the following comment on the rather friendly gesture of the Georgia Power Company (a private power company) in providing the group with free Coca-Colas:

> I also want to mention the fact that we were served Coca-Colas, which didn't impress me as being particularly ethical. As a matter of fact, I didn't like the whole idea of private power interest being represented. I learned nothing from this experience. Everyone at the plant looked like a miniature Wendell L. Willkie.

Thus does a strongly biased attitude invalidate judgment. Student number 44, whose scores were 3.9, 8.9, and 9.1, writes in her diary, "Many of our prejudices about private utilities were cleared up."

OPINIONS TEST

Table VII summarizes the results of the "before" and "after" opinions tests.

TABLE VII

OPINIONS TESTS

	Mean First Test	Mean Second Test	M_2-M_1	C. R.
Issue 1*....................	54.42	43.67	−9.75	4.08
Issue 2....................	48.17	50.00	1.83	.71
Issue 3....................	52.82	48.53	−4.30	1.76
Issue 4....................	53.03	51.00	−2.03	.61
Issue 5....................	47.91	54.46	6.55	1.74
Issue 6....................	51.65	48.62	−3.03	1.57
Issue 7....................	47.71	53.49	5.77	2.10

* Issues 1 to 7 are those stated in Chapter III.

Issue 1 tests an attitude similar to "unlimited individual initiative in farming" tested by the Kelley-Remmers scale. It will be noted that both measures show that the group changed reliably in the direction of becoming less favorable to the issue. In Chapter III it was stated that "The experimenter felt that the necessity of responding only to a list of predetermined statements (in the Kelley-Remmers Attitude Scale) might prevent the students from revealing their actual attitudes on the issues involved." This was one of the reasons for devising the Opinions Test. Since issue 1 of the Opinions Test, "An individual farmer should possess the sole right to make decisions in regard to the farming practice on his own farm," is almost identical with "institution" B (unlimited individual initiative in farming) of the Kelley-Remmers scale, correlation of the scores on these two tests should shed light on the validity of the two. Since the second application of the Kelley-Remmers scale, Form B, was given on February

10, and the second application of the Opinions Test was given at very nearly the same time (February 14), it was decided that these score distributions would be most valuable. *The correlation was .90.* This may be used to argue the validity of the Opinions Test, or of the use made of the Kelley-Remmers scale. The writer feels that the Opinions Test, with its freedom to make spontaneous response and with the evidence already submitted for the validity of the ranking technique employed, makes a satisfactory outside criterion to justify the argument that the use made of the generalized Kelley-Remmers Attitude Scale is valid. However, since these two instruments measured similar attitudes, at approximately the same time, using decidedly different techniques, and produced score distributions which correlated as highly as they did, it is logical to place more confidence in both of them.

Student number 15 has the following paragraph in his diary:

I was greatly interested in seeing this barren land with no soil except white sand. It particularly impresses one with the fact that the people are not able to control the land themselves but need government help. My view, that a farmer should have the sole right to make decisions concerning his land is changing rapidly. I see that in many cases the owners of the land are too uneducated to have any agricultural knowledge and that government interference is imperative in many cases in order to teach the farmer how to treat his land. I see more and more how poor land makes poor people and poor people make poor land and so on. The man Dr. Mitchell told us about (his father-in-law), who had unintentionally laid waste to such a large portion of this section was not a stupid man, but simply without any agricultural knowledge. If the government had been able to counsel him and help him get the most out of his land, we might not have viewed such a sandy waste this afternoon.

Unfortunately, the "before" score on this issue is missing. The "after" score is 44, indicating that student number 15 is more opposed to the issue than half the class. His Kelley-Remmers scores are 9.2, 9.5, and 8.7, indicating a change on the closely related issue which harmonizes with his diary statement.

Issue 2 tests an attitude similar to that measured by the Kelley-Remmers scale under the heading of socio-economic planning. It was argued above that the most reasonable interpretation of the data provided by the Kelley-Remmers scale on this issue was that the group was strongly in favor of socio-economic planning and remained so throughout. While issue 2 of the Opinions Test cannot bring evidence on the strength of the attitude, it does support the author's contention that no important change occurred. The attitude remained constant. This is shown by the low critical ratio of .71.

Student number 8, cited above as showing scores of 5.7, 9.5, and 9.7 on the Kelley-Remmers scale, shows a trend in the same direction on this scale. His scores are 50 and 58.

Student number 35 has the following statement in her diary:

I realized tonight, all of a sudden that this study is not merely an excuse for a trip, something to keep us busy until the end of the year, but a matter of great importance. Perhaps this matter of planning is the most important thing of our entire civilization.

Her Kelley-Remmers scores regarding socio-economic planning are 9.5, 9.8, and 9.8, indicating that she became more favorable to the kinds of planning defined. These test scores are consistent with her diary statement.

Issue 3 is similar to "Private Ownership of Utilities" of the Kelley-Remmers scale. The Opinions Test shows no statistically significant change. The comparable Kelley-Remmers means show a reliable change in the direction of becoming more favorable to private ownership of utilities. The Opinions Test shows an unreliable change which is, however, in the same direction; i.e., it shows the group to become less favorable to the government's entry into the power business. While these two tests are not identical, they are sufficiently related to warrant comparison.

Student number 17, cited above as expressing an attitude so strongly in opposition to private ownership of utilities that he resented free Coca-Colas, scores 48 and 48 on the two applications of the Opinions Test. This is about the mean for the group and does not indicate strong opposition to issue 5 as stated. Examination of his actual response to issue 3 reveals that he refuses to react because he feels that the government is not in competition with private power companies. His actual responses, in order, were:

1. I do not believe that competition is present where the government only rivals the private power interests. There cannot be competition unless the two adjoin. Just as two grocery stores at opposite ends of a town are not competitors.

2. I still contest the statement "in competition with" and refuse to believe that the government is competing with private power companies.

There is no change in opinion concerning issue 4. This issue did not come to the foreground of the group's experience.

No statistically significant change is found in the opinions concerning issues 5 and 6. With issue 7, although the change is not statistically significant according to the standard set, it is more reliable than the others and its direction is toward greater agreement with the issue as stated.

LAND MANAGEMENT TESTS

The three types of tests relative to land management produced results which are summarized in Table VIII.

TABLE VIII
LAND MANAGEMENT TESTS

	M_1 Test I	M_2 Test II	S. D. Test I	S. D. Test II	M_2-M_1	C. R.
Identification..........	32.91	40.94	12.32	5.11	8.03	4.12
Principles.............	18.94	48.80	12.90	17.91	29.86	3.34
Generalizations........	5.09	16.89	9.25	14.98	11.80	5.58

It will be observed that the group showed a reliable gain in ability to identify evidence of poor land management and procedures for better land management. If the study excursion truly "enriched the curriculum with realities, concretely experienced," one might expect the gain indicated.

In Chapter II, page 13, L. K. Frank [10 : 173] is quoted as saying that the essential task of general education is to convey some of the general ideas, meanings, and significances of the sciences. On page 14, the concern of general education with generalizations is noted. The statistically significant gains made by the group on the principles and generalizations tests indicate rather conclusively that the Lincoln School study excursion did achieve some of the purposes of general education. Perhaps the reader feels that the gains on the latter tests might have been greater. It should be remembered in this connection that no specific instruction in applying principles, nor in making generalizations was given. These gains are the result of the *experiences* of the study excursion without specific instruction in the processes tested. Further explanation will be given later.

POWER TESTS

Table IX summarizes the results of the tests for growth in ability to recognize the application of principles of power production and for growth in ability to generalize in regard to power production.

TABLE IX
POWER TESTS

	M_1 Test I	M_2 Test II	S. D. Test I	S. D. Test II	$M_2 - M_1$	C. R.
Principles.............	23.30	41.70	15.12	15.54	18.40	4.86
Generalizations........	2.44	6.88	4.71	4.99	4.44	3.48

These results indicate statistically significant gains. They thus are further evidence that the study excursion was a profitable technique for assisting students to form generalizations. They furnish further evidence for the achievement of some of the purposes of general education.

INTERRELATEDNESS OF SOME OUTCOMES

General education tends to regard learning as an integrated response to a pattern of experience. Learning is said to be integrated when the situation from which it arises is perceived as a meaningful whole. The learning situation can be perceived as a meaningful whole only if the various parts are perceived as interdependent or interrelated. Thus the philosophy of integration, an important part of the philosophy of general education, may be regarded as possible interrelatedness of the measured outcomes. Tables X and XI below were compiled in order to discover whether the learning experiences of the study excursion were such as to increase interrelatedness of some of the measured outcomes.

INTERRELATEDNESS AMONG KELLEY-REMMERS ATTITUDE SCORES

Table X summarizes the intercorrelations among the various attitudes. The "before" test is Form A, administered on January 3, and the "after" test is Form B, administered on February 10. It should be noted that the correlations between attitudes measured before the preparatory study and excursion are extremely low. The highest one is the negative correlation between unlimited individual initiative in farming and socio-economic planning. One might expect relationship between the attitudes toward unlimited individual initiative in farming and socio-economic planning, unlimited individual initiative in farming and private ownership of utilities, socio-economic planning and conservation, socio-economic planning and private ownership of utilities, at least. It will be observed that, with the exception of socio-economic planning and conservation (which show a considerably increased relationship in the "after" test), the correlations of these attitudes are among the highest shown. To the author, these low correlations indicate lack of sufficient knowledge upon the issues concerning which attitudes are expressed.

Although the differences between the "before" correlations and the "after" correlations are shown by the critical ratios to be unreliable according to the standard set on page 56, *it should be noted that the change is in a direction which indicates increased relationship.* Thus there is some evidence to indicate that the learning experiences of the study excursion increased the interrelatedness of some measured outcomes. The positive direction of the change in correlation between unlimited individual initiative in farming and socio-economic planning is surprising. The change in correlation between unlimited individual initiative in farming and private ownership of utilities is in a direction which indicates increased consistency and which results in the highest correlation reported. The highest critical ratio is reported for the change in correlation between socio-economic planning

TABLE X
Intercorrelations Among Kelley-Remmers Attitude Scores

Attitude	Before	After	Diff.	C. R.
Public relief and Unlimited individual initiative in farming	.02	.29	.27	1.26
Public relief and Socio-economic planning	.14	.23	.09	0.41
Public relief and Conservation	.07	.23	.16	0.73
Public relief and Private ownership of utilities	.16	.12	−.04	0.19
Unlimited individual initiative in farming and Socio-economic planning	−.33	−.03	+.30	1.38
Unlimited individual initiative in farming and Conservation	−.03	.06	.09	0.40
Unlimited individual initiative in farming and Private ownership of utilities	.29	.49	.20	1.04
Socio-economic planning and Conservation	−.05	.33	.38	1.76
Socio-economic planning and Private ownership of utilities	−.15	−.27	−.12	0.57
Conservation and Private ownership of utilities	−.06	.01	.07	0.30

Formulas used were:

$$r_{xy} = \frac{\frac{\Sigma xy}{N} - \bar{x}\bar{y}}{\sqrt{\frac{\Sigma x^2}{N} - (\bar{x})^2}\sqrt{\frac{\Sigma y^2}{N} - (\bar{y})^2}}.$$

To determine reliability of differences in correlations, r's were converted to Fisher's Z correlation functions using tables:

$$\sigma_z = \frac{1}{\sqrt{N-3}}$$

$$\sigma_{z_1 - z_2} = \sqrt{\sigma_{z_1}^2 + \sigma_{z_2}^2}$$

$$C. R. = \frac{Z_1 - Z_2}{\sigma_{z_1 - z_2}}$$

and conservation, and the positive sign of the "after" correlation seems to indicate a measure of consistency. The negative direction of the change in correlation between socio-economic planning and private ownership of utilities would again indicate a slight increase in consistency. The lack of reliability of the differences will leave these conclusions in regard to the changes open to question.

Interrelatedness Among Information, Principles, and Generalizations Scores

An attempt was made to study the change in relationship between students' information as measured by the information test and their ability to generalize and apply principles as measured by the land management and power tests. Unfortunately this attempt was not successful, owing to the fact that a number of individuals did not put enough effort into the test. These cases did not answer some of the principles test questions and did not respond to many of the requests to make generalizations. They are quite numerous, so that it is probably just to assume that the mean gains on the principles and generalizations tests should have been larger. They make invalid the correlation technique proposed as a method for studying the change in relationship between students' information and their ability to generalize and apply principles. The correlations are reported in Table XI, but no conclusions from the results are valid.

TABLE XI
Correlations between Information Scores, Principles Scores, and Generalizations Scores

Correlation	Before r	After r
Information and Land generalizations.....................	.47	.47
Information and Power generalizations....................	.28	.19
Information and Land principles.........................	.32	.40
Information and Power principles........................	.45	.08
Power generalizations and Power principles...............	.21	.31
Land generalizations and Land principles.................	.38	.17

Correlation between Teacher Ranking and Information Scores

The difference between the scores on information test number 1 and information test number 2 was computed for each student. The students were ranged according to these computed differences. The correlation between this ranking and the average of the teachers' rankings was computed, using the formula $r = 1 - \dfrac{6\Sigma D^2}{N(N^2 - 1)}$ where D is the difference in rank. The correlation was found to be $+.13$. It is positive, but very low, indicating very little relationship between the teachers' judgment and the ranking by gains in test scores.

CORRELATION BETWEEN TEACHER RANKING AND RANKING ACCORDING TO CHANGE IN ATTITUDE

The students were ranked according to their change in attitude toward unlimited individual initiative in farming. This ranking was correlated with the teachers' ranking of the students according to gain in information. The correlation was $-.17$. This is so low that it indicates no relationship.

It is frequently argued that teachers who are working steadily with boys and girls can estimate very reliably gain in information and changes in attitude. The teachers of Lincoln School who participated in this study excursion were certainly working steadily with the students and they are among the better teachers of the country. Yet their estimate of gains in information and the gains as shown by the information test bear little relationship. Little relationship is shown also between the changes in one attitude as measured by the Kelley-Remmers Attitude Scale and the change according to teachers' estimates. Since inconsistency exists, either the tests or the teachers are unreliable. Evidence for the reliability and validity of the Kelley-Remmers test has been submitted. It would appear then that there is little truth in the statement that teachers can reliably estimate information gains and attitude changes, even when the association is as close as it was on the Lincoln School study excursion.

CORRELATION BETWEEN RANKING BY GAIN ON THE INFORMATION TEST AND RANKING BY CHANGE IN ATTITUDE

The same ranking according to change in attitude toward unlimited individual initiative in farming, described above, was correlated with the ranking according to computed gains in information scores. The correlation was —.50. This indicates that, to a considerable degree, gain in information as measured by the information test is associated with increased opposition to unlimited individual initiative in farming.

ANALYSIS OF GAINS MADE BY THREE ABILITY GROUPS

Some educators feel that excursions provide experiences so concrete that students with relatively little verbal ability may profit more than students with superior verbal ability. It may be argued that students who have considerable ability to profit from vicarious experience lose interest in real experience because of the maze of subsidiary ideas, irrelevant to the main thought, which always accompany real experiences. Loss of interest will probably be followed by loss of profit from the experience. On the other hand, vicarious experiences, presented in symbolic form by competent authors, will eliminate irrelevant ideas and keep subsidiary ideas in their proper relation to the whole thought. Students who have superior ability to work with such symbolic representations of experience will be so used to doing so that they may be placed at a disadvantage when confronted with the irrelevancies, inconsistencies, and delays of real experience. Students with inferior ability to profit from academic and abstract subjects may, on the other hand, deal more competently with real experiences because they are more used to doing so. Such students cannot find the satisfaction of achievement in abstract subjects. They are forced to find such satisfaction through achievement in concrete, real experiences. Thus, because they have had more practice in dealing with realities, they may be more competent to profit from real experiences than students with greater academic ability.

Other educators feel that the students with superior ability in abstract and academic subjects can profit most from any experience, real or vicarious. They argue that such students, because of their greater ability to detect central ideas and to follow trends of thought, will be able to disregard irrelevancies more successfully than students with lesser academic ability. The academically superior students will have greater success in keeping subsidiary ideas in their proper relation to the main theme. They will be able to sustain their interest over longer periods of time. Thus they will be able to profit from real experiences more than students with less academic ability, in spite of the fact that they probably are less practiced in dealing with realities.

The problems with which this section deals may be stated as follows: (1) If students are divided into three groups according to their abstract academic ability, which group will gain most from the real experiences of a study excursion? (2) Which of the three groups described above will change their attitudes and opinions most, as a result of the study excursion?

Evidence relative to these problems was obtained by dividing the forty-six participating students into three groups according to their scores on the American Council on Education Psychological Test, a test primarily of verbal intelligence. Group one consisted of the fifteen students with the highest scores. Group two consisted of the sixteen students with intermediate scores. Group three consisted of the fifteen students with the lowest scores. The mean gain of each of these groups was computed for each outcome where the entire class showed reliable change. When calculating changes in attitude and opinion, signs were neglected. This means that the figures are a measure of the change in attitude and opinion regardless of direction of change. They will answer the question of which group showed most change in attitude and opinion as a result of the study excursion. The results are shown in Table XII.

Examination of the row showing average gains on the first six tests of Table XII reveals that the group with superior academic ability gained more from the study excursion than the other two groups, and that the middle group gained more than the lowest group. Evidently students with superior ability in academic and abstract subjects, as indicated by superior scores on the American Council on Education Psychological Test, profit more from the real experiences of a study excursion than do the less gifted students. The lowest group shows superior gain in ability to identify. Perhaps it gained most in the relatively simple process of identification, while the groups with superior ability gained most when the process was more complicated.

Examination of the average change in attitude and opinion indicates that group one changed more than the other two groups and that group three changed least. Students with superior academic and abstract ability, as indicated by superior scores on the American Council on Education Psychological Test, show a greater tendency than less gifted students to change their attitudes and opinions as a result of the real experiences of a study excursion.

This analysis provides evidence in support of the position taken by educators who argue that students with superior ability in abstract and academic subjects can profit more from the concrete experiences of a study excursion than students with inferior ability. Change in attitude

TABLE XII

GAINS AND CHANGES MADE BY THREE ABILITY GROUPS

Test	Group One	Group Two	Group Three
Information Test..........................	29.4	32.8	26.5
Land Management Identification Test........	6.9	6.8	10.3
Land Principles Test.......................	35.3	27.5	26.5
Land Generalizations Test..................	13.7	13.7	8.1
Power Principles Test......................	18.6	18.3	19.6
Power Generalizations Test.................	5.2	6.1	1.4
Average Gain on First Six Tests of This Table.	18.2	17.5	15.4
Attitude Re Unlimited Individual Initiative in Farming...............................	2.3	2.6	1.5
Attitude Re Private Ownership of Utilities...	1.5	1.9	1.8
Opinion Re: An Individual Farmer Should Possess the Sole Right to Make Decisions in Regard to the Farming Practice on His Own Farm..................................	14.2	12.9	12.4
Average Change in Attitude and Opinion....	6.0	5.8	5.2

and opinion regarding important public issues may be considered a real gain. In this sense, too, the students with superior abstract ability profit most from the concrete experiences of a study excursion.

EVIDENCE OF GROWTHS INDICATED BUT NOT MEASURED

Critical thinking is indicated by the following quotation from the diary of student number 34:

Sunday afternoon we went out to the dam in our buses, and all were amazed at its size. Everything was modern, huge, sharp, clean and definite.

We were surrounded by inhumanity in the form of turbines. The whole thing was frightfully depressing—I don't know why, but I have tried to analyze my reaction. Was it that I saw in this project the goal toward which mankind is moving—everything precise and clock-like, working together at highest efficiency, organized, planned, orderly? And was it the submersion of the individual, a future state in which everyone is alike and perfectly fitted into the scheme of things, doing a part and then going? Perhaps that was what made me want to run out to the wind away from a scientifically beautiful world. But how can it be, when I believe in planning, think the T. V. A. is splendid? It is a huge question and one that I cannot hope to be consistent about.

Critical thinking in regard to important social issues is evidenced by the following quotation from the diary of student number 29:

It is rather difficult to compare the merits of public and private utilities companies because their aims are really so widely separated. The man who explained the Georgia Power Company said, "The T. V. A. is not doing anything that our company hasn't done for the last fifteen years." That's obviously not true—in the first place, a private company hasn't the facilities to carry out a program such as the T. V. A. has inaugurated and in the second place, power is the chief consideration with a private company and everything else is secondary.

Information and appreciation which may help to realize the potentialities of the learner in reference to the needs of the society that is and that is to be is evidenced by the following from the diary of student number 42:

What I can't see is how the people get a living out of the land in some of the places we went through. It was barren and had a great deal of soil erosion. The land looked poor and in need of fertilizer. For the first time I actually see what they mean by soil erosion.

Evidence of adjustment in personal relations is provided by the following from the diary of student number 5:

Something must have hit me because I danced with a girl for the first time in my life! However, my primary occupation was getting acquainted with people—I got to know at least seven—all of them really nice too.

Evidence of reflective thinking is illustrated by the following quotation from the diary of student number 25:

G. and H. wanted to make of him a libertine and an atheist, but I think they are wrong. I would rather permit him to become a saint—a sort of Pietra Spina of religion, but of course M. will never be that. He has not enough of the stuff that makes a saint question before he will believe. You should have skepticism before you can have fanatical conviction—and I think, though I did compose it myself, that this wise dictum is true.

The study excursion purports to vitalize the emotional content of units of work. Some evidence of this is contained in the following excerpts from the diary of student number 37:

I tried to sketch but I couldn't. I think I even fell asleep, sitting on the trunks and branches of pine trees. Next moment I knew that somebody was watching me very closely. I opened my eyes and there was a woman with a child on her arm. I remembered I saw her down in the farm house. She shyly smiled at me and said that she was admiring my unfinished sketch. She was very awkward and shy, but friendly, and she made me (to my surprise), talk about myself and art. I couldn't understand that a poor, hard-working farmer would know anything about drawing and painting, but she did. She had always wanted to have colors and be an artist, but never had any opportunity and time to, and never will, she added sadly, with a faint smile.

The sun didn't shine so brightly, suddenly. The grass was brown. There were clouds on the sky. The pine trees were crooked. I don't think I liked Georgia at that moment. I felt bitterly what it means to want something and never get it. I wouldn't be able to live if I couldn't sketch, and she must have felt the same way. How unfair.

SUMMARY

The results of the testing program have been reported, together with interpretations of them. Some of the diary excerpts and the author's personal observations have been reported.

In general the evidence submitted supports the thesis that the study excursion is one procedure for implementation of the philosophy of general education. A large reliable gain in information, as measured by the information test, was reported. An attitude of mild approval toward the institution of public relief was revealed. It did not show reliable change throughout the study excursion. The attitude of the group toward unlimited individual initiative in farming is shown to change in the direction of becoming less favorable. The most reasonable interpretation of the results of the attitude tests concerning socio-economic planning is that the group were strongly in favor of socio-economic planning before the study excursion and remained so throughout. The group's attitude toward conservation remained consistently favorable. The change in attitude toward private ownership of utilities, over the entire period of the study excursion, is reliable and indicates lessened opposition to private ownership of utilities.

On issue 1 of the Opinions Test the group revealed reliable change in the direction of becoming less favorable. This checks with the results of the Kelley-Remmers test for attitude toward unlimited individual initiative in farming. Evidence has been submitted to support the writer's use of the generalized Kelley-Remmers Attitude Scale for a specific purpose and to lend confidence to the belief in the validity of the Kelley-Remmers Scale and the Opinions Test. The attitude toward issue 2 of the Opinions Test remained unchanged. The results for issue 3 indicate no statistically significant change in the mean of the group's attitudes. No reliable change in attitude toward issues 4, 5, 6, and 7 can be reported. When the change is not reliable the direction of the change may still be interesting, and some attempt to interpret these data has been made. Reliable gains were shown in ability to identify evidence of poor land management and procedures for better land management, ability to recognize the application of principles, and ability to generalize. These gains, and the changes in attitude, indicate that the study excursion achieved some of the purposes of general education.

An attempt was made to determine whether the learning experiences of the study excursion were such as to increase the interrelatedness of some of the measured outcomes. Intercorrelations between the scores on the Kelley-Remmers Attitude Scale were extremely low before the trip. In general, the correlations after the trip were higher, indicating a trend toward increased interrelatedness; but the changes in correlation cannot be described as reliable. No conclusions can be drawn from the correlations between various combinations of information scores, principles scores, and generalizations scores.

Very little relation was found between the teachers' ranking of students in order of gain in information and ranking of students according to gains shown on the information test. It should be noted in this connection that all the teachers who co-operated by attempting to rank the students felt that the task was too difficult and that their rankings would not be reliable. However, it appears that there is little truth in the statement that teachers can reliably estimate information gains and attitude changes, even when they are very closely associated with their students.

There was considerably more relationship between the ranking according to gains on the information test and the ranking by change in attitude than there was between the ranking by teachers and the ranking by change in attitude.

CHAPTER V

SUMMARY AND CONCLUSIONS

THIS study has provided some evidence that the study excursion, as an educational enterprise, is capable of producing outcomes in addition to gains in factual knowledge, outcomes which current educational theory is emphasizing as increasingly important. It may be justly claimed that the study excursion is an effective procedure for bringing "the individual into contact with the culture which is his birthright in such fashion as to widen and deepen his consciousness of his relation to the life of the past, the present, and the future, and to aid in the development of those attributes which are most needed if he is to play intelligently his personal role in the drama of cultural continuance and cultural change." [21 : 8]

The study excursion is an educational procedure in which information about subject matter and skill in manipulation of subject matter are not glorified as the only or as the primary objectives of educational experiences. In the study excursion, the outcomes of which have been reported, understandings in generalizations and in application of principles, and attitudes, appreciations, and interests of the learner in relation to his society have been considered as essential objectives of the experience. Furthermore, evidence indicating that progress toward the achievement of these objectives was made through the medium of the study excursion has been presented. Information, attitudes, opinions, generalizations, application of principles, appreciation, critical thinking, and adjustment in personal relations have all been influenced by the study excursion and in such a way that there was a maximum chance for enthusiasms and purposes to be kindled.

In Chapter II certain specific questions were raised. The investigation was planned to gather evidence which might answer them. Specific conclusions of the study will be stated as answers to those questions. See pages 24 and 25 for question one.

The following reliable growths and changes have been reported: A marked growth in understanding of the problems of soil erosion, and land management, and of the procedures used to convert energy of falling water into useful electrical energy; a change in attitude indicating that the group became less favorably disposed toward unlimited individual initiative in farming; a change in attitude indicating that the group became more favorably disposed toward private ownership of utilities; a change in opinion which indicated that the group became less favorably disposed to the proposition that an individual farmer should possess the sole right to make decisions in regard to the farming practice on his own farm; a growth in the group's ability to identify evidence of poor land management and procedures for better land management; a growth in the group's ability to recognize the application of principles of land management; a growth in the group's ability to recognize the application of principles of power production; a growth in the group's ability to generalize in regard to land management; a growth in the group's ability to generalize in regard to power production. Other possible outcomes listed did not show statistically reliable growth or change. Anecdotal and diary evidence has been submitted to indicate that there are beneficial changes in some people in critical thinking and appreciation and in adjustment in personal relations.

In answer to question two, "What is the relationship between teachers' opinions of students' attitudes and attitudes as shown by objective measurement?" the author must report failure to gather evidence because most of the teachers did not get an opportunity to give their "before" judgment.

In answer to question three, "What is the relationship between teachers' estimate of information gains and gains shown by objective measurement?", it has been shown that there is little relationship. It would appear that teachers cannot reliably estimate information gain.

In answer to question four, "Are the learning experiences of the study excursion such as to increase interrelatedness among attitudes?" it has been shown that there was a change in the direction of increased relationship among the attitudes measured. The amount of the change, however, is not sufficient with respect to errors of measurement, or of sampling, to allow for the generalization that such changes may be expected in this sample in other fields, or in similar samples in the same fields.

In answer to question five, "Are there changes in relationship between students' information and their ability to generalize and to apply principles?" the author must report failure to gather conclusive evidence because a number of students did not put enough effort into the second tests. From this experience it becomes clear that evaluation studies should avoid the error of overtesting.

In answer to question six, "Is there any relationship between gain in information and change in attitude?" it has been shown that to a considerable degree gain in information as measured by the information test is associated with increased opposition to unlimited individual initiative in farming.

In answer to question seven, "If the participants in the excursion are divided into three groups according to ability, which group will profit most from the experiences of the excursion?" it has been shown that, on the whole, the group with superior ability profited most from the study excursion. The exception is the case of the ability to identify. The upper ability group showed a greater tendency to change their attitudes as a result of study excursion experiences.

The Lincoln School Study Excursion was costly. While this is true, the outcomes demonstrated for this excursion probably can be obtained from less costly excursions, as long as such excursions fall within the definition of study excursions given in this report. This conclusion, however, cannot be completely proved as the findings can be generalized only to groups like the Lincoln School group and to excursions like the Lincoln School Excursion.

From examination of the demonstrated outcomes, it would appear to the author that all conditions of the study excursion being equal to those reported, the best single measure of the value and worth of a study excursion is the increase in knowledge or information. However, it should be noted carefully that "all conditions of the study excursion being equal" means that the knowledge or information measured *be not mere memorized information.* Obviously increased information, as measured by the information test, could be achieved through study of the subjects in the classroom, or by memorization of the accepted answers. If increase in information resulted from such procedures rather than from the natural experiences of a study excursion, there is no reason to believe that it is an indication of the other important outcomes with which this report is concerned.

In Chapter II, under the heading of general education, it will be noted that outcomes such as the ones just described for the Lincoln School study excursion are among the major aims of general education. The writer feels justified in the assertion that evidence in support of the claim that the study excursion is one method for implementation of the general education philosophy has been submitted.

John Dewey [7 : 367–369] is quoted in Chapter II as stressing the evils of isolating subjects from their social setting. Clearly, this study excursion was not guilty of that error. Many subjects and topics were studied, but in every case the subject matter and the purpose for studying it were deeply imbedded in their vitalizing social setting. The social setting provided both the purpose of, and the justification for, the effort displayed. The very nature of the study excursion, as defined for this report, makes isolation of subjects from their social setting difficult and unnatural. The study excursion may be judged to be a valuable instrument of general education.

RECOMMENDATIONS RE FURTHER RESEARCH

1. A rewarding study might be made of the relationship and change in relationship between information concerning social issues and attitudes toward those issues.

2. A study designed to evaluate information growths in fields other than science should prove valuable.

3. The technique for evaluating ability to generalize, growth in ability to generalize, ability to apply principles, and growth in ability to apply principles, established by this study, might be used in fields other than science, and might be applied to other proposed objectives of general education.

4. A controlled experimental study planned to determine whether classroom study or a study excursion is more effective as a means of developing ability to generalize should prove valuable.

SELECTED BIBLIOGRAPHY

1. ALLPORT, GORDON W. AND VERNON, PHILIP E. *Studies in Expressive Movement.* New York: The Macmillan Company, 1933.
2. ARNOLD, HERBERT J. *The Selection, Organization and Evaluation of Localities Available for Unspecialized Field Work in Earth Science in the New York City Region.* The author, 1936.
3. ATYEO, HENRY C. *The Excursion as a Teaching Technique.* Contributions to Education, No. 761. New York: Teachers College, Columbia University, 1938.
4. BAKER, G. DERWOOD. *Report on The Lincoln School Study Excursion* (In preparation). New York: Teachers College, Columbia University, 1938.
5. BRYAN, H. ELOISE. *Out of the Classroom into Life.* The National Elementary Principal, Bulletin of the Department of Elementary School Principals, National Education Association. Vol. 13, pp. 278-283, June, 1934.
6. CRAWFORD, C. C. AND GRINSTEAD, ROLAND W. "The Use of the Excursion in Teaching Commercial Geography." *Journal of Geography,* Vol. 29, pp. 301–306, October, 1930.
7. DEWEY, JOHN. "What Is Social Study?" *Progressive Education,* Vol. 15, pp. 367–369, May, 1938.
8. DEWEY, JOHN, CHILDS, JOHN L., AND OTHERS. *The Educational Frontier.* New York: The Century Co., 1933.
9. DIX, LESTER. "Integration in the Lincoln School Philosophy." *Teachers College Record,* Vol. 37, pp. 363–371, 1936.
10. FRANK, L. K. "The Task of General Education." *The Social Frontier,* Vol. 3, pp. 171-173, March, 1937.
11. FULCOMER, EDWIN S. "American Culture." *Teachers College Record,* Vol. 37, pp. 422–426, February, 1936.
12. GREAT PLAINS COMMITTEE. *The Future of the Great Plains.* Washington, D. C.: Superintendent of Documents, U. S. Government Printing Office, 1936.
13. GRINSTEAD, ROLAND H. "An Experimental Evaluation of the School Excursion." University of Southern California Master's Thesis, June, 1929.
14. HOBEN, CHARLES F. "English and German Students Make Long Trips at Low Cost." *School Life,* Vol. 16, pp. 146–147, April, 1931.
15. HULL, CLARK L. *Aptitude Testing.* New York: World Book Co., 1928.

16. KANDEL, I. L. *Comparative Education.* Boston: Houghton Mifflin Co., 1933.
17. KELLEY, IDA B. *The Construction and Evaluation of a Scale to Measure Attitude Toward Any Institution.* Studies in Higher Education XXVI, Bulletin of Purdue University, December, 1934.
18. KELLEY, IDA B. AND REMMERS, H. H. *A Scale for Measuring Attitude Toward Any Institution.* West Lafayette, Indiana: Purdue Research Foundation, 1934.
19. PERSON, H. S. *Little Waters;* A study of headwater streams and other little waters, their use and relations to the land. Washington, D. C.: Superintendent of Documents, U. S. Government Printing Office, 1936.
20. POWERS, S. R. AND OTHERS. *A Program for Teaching Science.* National Society for the Study of Education, Thirty-first Yearbook, Part I. Bloomington, Ill.: Public School Publishing Co., 1932.
21. POWERS, S. R. (Chairman). "Progress Report of a Committee Appointed to Consider a Projected Proposal for an Enlarged Program for General Education." Mimeographed report. Teachers College, Columbia University, January 14, 1937; Supplementary and Revised Material, December 29, 1937.
22. POWERS, S. R. AND OTHERS. "Preliminary Statement Regarding the Conference on a Proposed Journal of General Education Called at Minneapolis on June 26th and 27th, 1937." Mimeographed material. Teachers College, Columbia University.
23. PRICE, R. H. "A Study of the Values of Field Trips." *The National Elementary Principal,* Bulletin of the Department of Elementary School Principals, National Education Association, Vol. 13, pp. 302-305, June, 1934.
24. SNEDECOR, GEORGE W. *Statistical Methods.* Menasha, Wisconsin: Collegiate Press, 1938.

VITA

James Anderson Fraser was born in Kroonstad, Orange Free State, Union of South Africa, on March 18, 1907. His elementary school education was obtained in various parts of the Province of Alberta, Canada, and in Seattle, Washington. His high school education was obtained in Victoria High School, Edmonton, Alberta, Canada.

After leaving high school Mr. Fraser trained as a telegrapher but never worked at the vocation. He attended the Camrose Normal School in Alberta, and graduated with a first class Alberta Teaching Certificate. His first school was a rural one in which all grades from one to nine were represented by one or two children. The next year he became principal of a rural high school. The following year (1928–1929) he was appointed to the staff of the city of Edmonton, as a grade teacher. From 1929 until 1935 he attended summer schools at the University of Alberta. In the fall of 1929 he was appointed critic teacher in the training school of the Edmonton Normal School, in Edmonton, Alberta. After two years' experience in that capacity he enrolled in "honors chemistry" at the University of Alberta for the degree of B.Sc. The degree was granted in 1933. For the next three years Mr. Fraser was vice-principal of one of the Edmonton schools and instructor in science during the summer sessions at the University of Alberta. During these years he assisted in the revision of the Alberta Course of Study and wrote large portions of the course for elementary and junior high school science. He was one of the group responsible for organizing the "enterprise" program in Alberta, which is a modified "experience" curriculum.

After attending one summer session (1935) at Teachers College, Columbia University, Mr. Fraser won a $1000 Teachers College Fellowship, which enabled him to complete the work for the A.M. degree in science education at Teachers College. He was president of the Science Club, a member of the student council, and elected to membership in Phi Delta Kappa. He is a member of Delta Upsilon fraternity and a Mason.

The year after obtaining the A.M. degree Mr. Fraser won a $400 Naomi Norsworthy scholarship from Teachers College, Columbia University, and an appointment as Research Assistant in the Advanced School of Education, Teachers College, Columbia.

Mr. Fraser is employed at present in the State Teachers College at Bemidji, Minnesota.

VITA

James Anderson Fraser was born in Kroonstad, Orange Free State, Union of South Africa, on March 18, 1907. His elementary school education was obtained in various parts of the Province of Alberta, Canada, and in Seattle, Washington. His high school education was obtained in Victoria High School, Edmonton, Alberta, Canada.

After leaving high school Mr. Fraser trained as a telegrapher but never worked at the vocation. He attended the Camrose Normal School in Alberta, and graduated with a first class Alberta Teaching Certificate. His first school was a rural one in which all grades from one to nine were represented by one or two children. The next year he became principal of a rural high school. The following year (1928–1929) he was appointed to the staff of the city of Edmonton, as a grade teacher. From 1929 until 1935 he attended summer schools at the University of Alberta. In the fall of 1929 he was appointed critic teacher in the training school of the Edmonton Normal School, in Edmonton, Alberta. After two years' experience in that capacity he enrolled in "honors chemistry" at the University of Alberta for the degree of B.Sc. The degree was granted in 1933. For the next three years Mr. Fraser was vice-principal of one of the Edmonton schools and instructor in science during the summer sessions at the University of Alberta. During these years he assisted in the revision of the Alberta Course of Study and wrote large portions of the course for elementary and junior high school science. He was one of the group responsible for organizing the "enterprise" program in Alberta, which is a modified "experience" curriculum.

After attending one summer session (1935) at Teachers College, Columbia University, Mr. Fraser won a $1000 Teachers College Fellowship, which enabled him to complete the work for the A.M. degree in science education at Teachers College. He was president of the Science Club, a member of the student council, and elected to membership in Phi Delta Kappa. He is a member of Delta Upsilon fraternity and a Mason.

The year after obtaining the A.M. degree Mr. Fraser won a $400 Naomi Norsworthy scholarship from Teachers College, Columbia University, and an appointment as Research Assistant in the Advanced School of Education, Teachers College, Columbia.

Mr. Fraser is employed at present in the State Teachers College at Bemidji, Minnesota.

Mr. Fraser has had a number of science articles for children published in *The Children's Magazine* by "The Institute of Applied Arts" in Edmonton, Alberta, Canada. He is the author of a number of study guides designed to accompany the science sound films sold by the ERPI Classroom Films, Inc.